Legally Mom

REAL WOMEN'S STORIES OF BALANCING MOTHERHOOD & LAW PRACTICE

anne murphy brown

Legally Mom

REAL WOMEN'S STORIES OF BALANCING MOTHERHOOD & LAW PRACTICE

anne murphy brown

Printed in the United States of America.

16 15 14 13 12 5 4 3 2 1

Library of Congress Cataloging-in-Publication Data

Brown, Anne Murphy.
   Legally mom : real women's stories of balancing motherhood and law practice / by Anne Murphy Brown.—1st ed.
      p. cm.
   Includes bibliographical references.
   ISBN 978-1-61438-512-7 (print : alk. paper)
1. Women lawyers—United States. 2. Working mothers—United States. I. Title.
   KF299.W6B76 2012
   340.092'520973—dc23

                                                                        2012020468

CONTENTS

Part Five—Setting Up a Law Practice—Hanging Out a Shingle

Part Six—The Road Less Travelled

DEDICATION

For my husband, Chris
and our children,
Caroline, William and their
little brother or sister on the way.

ACKNOWLEDGMENTS

This book would not have been possible without the tremendous support of friends, family and colleagues over the last two years. My husband, Chris, has patiently listened to me talk about the topic of working parenthood for the last six years and I would like to thank him for always believing in this project. I would also like to thank my sweet children, Caroline and William, for whom words cannot describe my love. I would like to especially thank my sister Eileen for being a model of motherhood, a sounding board on this topic and a proofreader of my first chapter. My parents, Jerome and Carol Murphy, deserve special thanks for emotional and educational support throughout my life. My sibling's success and love has always been an inspiration, especially my sister Katherine and brother Bill, who have dedicated their lives to education. I could not have completed this book, or anything else professionally, without the help of Amy Melvin covering the home front. I owe her a depth of gratitude for the wonderful care she has given my children.

Further thanks goes to my sister-in-law, Katie Murphy, and friends Maureen Juskaitis and Beth Vlerick, who generously made connections to women interviewed for this project. In addition, I would like to extend a special thanks to Joan Burda for putting me in touch with ABA Publishing and explaining the publishing process. I would also like to thank Dee Dee Bober, for acting as an early proofreader.

I am forever grateful to Erin Nevius, Executive Editor at ABA Publishing, who championed this book for her patience and encouragement throughout the entire project.

I would like to express my gratitude to the faculty, administration, staff and students of Ursuline College, especially Dr. JoAnne Podis and Dr. Debra Fleming who supported my research agenda on the topic of motherhood and the legal profession from its inception. Special thanks to Katie Cirincione for cheering me on throughout this process.

A number of other organizations have been instrumental throughout this process, including: the American Association for Paralegal Education, who supported my research by assisting me in making connections across the country; Brande Stellings at Catalyst for talking with me about further research and women in the legal profession; the San Francisco Bar Association – No Glass Ceiling Initiative, Women Lawyers Association of Michigan-Oakland County Region, the Association of Black Women Lawyers of New Jersey, all of whom sent out information to their members about my research; the website, Ms.JD for allowing me to post information about my project; and Peter Krouse of the *Cleveland Plain Dealer* for mentioning my book and research in his article on women in the judiciary.

Last, but not least, I would like to thank the women who were interviewed for this book. They gave their time, their stories, their trust and their encouragement to me as a stranger writing about a topic that they felt was important enough to warrant reflection and contribution. To these women, Tracy Betz, Elizabeth McBride, Dyan Finguerra-DuCharme, Kristen Pursley, Kristie Cary Fingerhut, Nikki Hudman, Anne-Marie Kennedy, Ama Romaine, Barbara Rogan, Maggie Harris, Tara Ori, Stacey Ferguson, Nadia Jones, Rona Kaufman Kitchen, Alexandra Foote, Jill Krolikowski, Vy Nguyen, Kathleen Havener, Maureen Pikarski, Alice Bruno, Donna Peel, Sheila Pont, Jenny Brody, Gwen Norgle-Reedy, and the Honorable Patricia A. Gaughan, I am so grateful.

Introduction

THERE IS AN OBVIOUS GENDER GAP within the legal profession. According to the Bureau of Labor Statistics, in 2010, women made up 31.9% of all lawyers.[1] The ironic thing is that since 1986, ABA-approved law schools have consistently graduated between 40% and 50% women.[2] Not being a statistician myself, I still look at these numbers and wonder—where are the rest of the female lawyers going?

Unfortunately, few have headed to the upper echelons of the legal profession. Less than 16% of equity partners in law firms and only 20% of general counsels at Fortune 500 companies are women.[3] The bottom

---

1. Bureau of Labor Statistics, *Household Data Annual Averages, 2010, available at* http://www.bls.gov/cps/cpsaat11.pdf (last visited April 18, 2012).

2. American Bar Association, *Legal Education Statistics from ABA-Approved Law Schools, J.D. and LL.B. Degrees Awarded, 1981–2010, available at* http://www.americanbar.org/content/dam/aba/administrative/legal_education_and_admissions_to_the_bar/stats_7.authcheckdam.pdf (last visited April 18, 2012).

3. Catalyst Report 2012, *Women in the Law in the U.S., available at* http://catalyst.org/file/554/qt_women_in_law_in_the_us.pdf (last visited April 18, 2012).

line also reflects this disparity—female lawyers generally made only 77% of male lawyer salaries in 2010.[4]

As a young attorney, gender issues should have been more apparent to me as I began to navigate my own legal career. As I practiced with a law firm, meeting attorneys from other firms and through the bar association, it was generally evident that there were more men than women in the profession, especially in coveted management roles. I particularly chose a firm that had female partners with strong reputations in the legal community. I really didn't see the issues with the gender gap until I started thinking about motherhood. As I started down that road, I looked around and noticed that though there were few women in leadership positions, there were even fewer that had children or had much to do with child rearing. Statistically, this perception rang true, as approximately 25% of women lawyers leave the legal profession once they have children.[5]

For several reasons, including motherhood, I chose to transition to an academic career: however, the question still nagged at me. How does motherhood impact a woman's career as a lawyer? What part does motherhood play in the attrition of female lawyers? And, from a practical standpoint, how can a woman succeed in the law while also having children?

I have not attempted to answer these questions quantitatively. Those statistics are for someone with a far more mathematical mind than mine. What I have attempted to do with *Legally Mom*, is give a snapshot of legal moms around the country, working at firms, corporations, governmental entities, and nonprofits, and profiling their careers and the impact of motherhood. I particularly wanted to know what challenges they have faced and how they have dealt with the competing demands of a career in the law and raising children.

---

4. Bureau of Labor Statistics, Current Population Survey, "Table 39: Median weekly earnings of full-time wage and salary workers by detailed occupation and sex," Annual Averages 2010, available at ftp://ftp.bls.gov/pub/special.requests/lf/aa2010/pdf/cpsaat39.pdf (last visited April 18, 2012).

5. ABA Journal, *About Twenty-Five Percent of Lawyer Moms Leave the Workplace, Study Finds, Debra Cassens Weiss, May 9, 2011, available at* http://www.abajournal.com/news/article/25_percent_of_lawyer_moms_leave_the_workplace_study_finds/ (last visited April 18, 2012).

If you have picked up this book, chances are you are a mom, or thinking about becoming a mom, or someone concerned about the intersection of motherhood and the practice of law. *Legally Mom* profiles mothers in different stages of their legal careers with children of varied ages. As someone who has wrestled with the big questions related to career and motherhood, I sought advice from women who had been there and could provide some perspective on their experience. In addition, I hope this book helps attorneys who are also raising children to know that they are not alone in this endeavor. As a society, we have a vested interest in how each generation is fostered and developed, but this is easy to forget as pressures mount over billable hours and client demands.

I sought to interview women who were not only honest with me but honest with themselves—women who were willing to share the good times and the bad. The days when their child screamed, "Mommy, don't go!" at the daycare, the days when the appellate brief was submitted with macaroni and cheese stuck to the bottom, and those golden days when everything felt liked it clicked into place. The 25 women who participated in interviews for this book were inspirational and thought provoking. Their candor and willingness to share their experiences demonstrate the best of female camaraderie. To say that I am grateful for their participation is not enough: I am truly humbled by their accomplishments and kindness. Many, many thanks.

These are their stories. . . .

Part One

LAW FIRM LIVING

Chapter One

CLIMBING THE LADDER IN HIGH HEELS TOTING A DIAPER BAG

"You feel like you are actually doing something for the first time in your life that really matters."

—*Tracy Betz*

To say that Tracy Betz is driven would be an understatement. As an attorney living and working in Indianapolis, her focus on her career is akin to Jeff Gordon driving the Indianapolis 500. Tracy has been a litigator for the last seven years. She is also a mother of a two and a half year old daughter and newly pregnant with her second child. She is in the final climb toward partnership and highly focused on her goal, as she has been her entire life.

At five years old, Tracy visited Disney World with her family and specifically went to the Hall of Presidents. It struck her that all of the presidents were men. When she asked her father why, he responded that it was because she was going to be the first woman president; but, he said, she had to be a lawyer first. Agreeing with his logic, Tracy said, "Okay, I will be a lawyer first," and she never wavered from this aspiration. However, she did abandon her original plan to be the leader of the free world. She is a litigator and very active in her local Democratic Party.

Her academic choices supported her ultimate goal. In high school she focused on courses that were history based, especially American History. She also participated in a Street Law class, which exposed her to American government and legal issues. She attended Indiana University at Bloomington, majoring in Political Science and Gender Studies, minoring in Sociology. During her college years she focused on courses that would prepare her for the rigor of law school, even taking a course in the Philosophy Department that exposed her to legal logical reasoning that would come in handy on the LSAT. She graduated college a full year early so that she could begin law school sooner.

Tracy enjoyed law school at Indiana University, especially discussing the cases and their nuances. Being in practice now, she misses the classroom dialogues and differences of opinion encouraged in academia. She admits that law school was intense—being thrown into a classroom with all overachievers was a new experience. Ultimately, someone has to be at the top and someone is at the bottom when grades come due. Situations structured this way, such as law firm billing, still seem to give Tracy anxiety. She worries about ever being considered mediocre in any respect.

Even during her formative years in education, Tracy knew she wanted to both work and be a mom. She also realized that it was not going to be easy. Her knowledge of feminist literature as a Gender Studies major formed her familiarity with the struggles of working mothers. Tracy remarked, "It was something that I was concerned about, but I was determined that it was something that I would make work and I could make work."

Although she was aware of the perils of working moms, when she sought out her first job while in law school, she did not take into consideration any work-life balance issues. She describes herself as "naïve" in her early twenties.

> When I was looking for jobs, I didn't specifically look for a firm based on quality of life, because you get so caught up with what is the best

firm that wants me. It's just a really weird process that you lose sight of what really matters to you because they are offering you so much money or it is so prestigious to be interviewed by this firm or that firm. I didn't think about it during the interview process actually at all. Once you are at your law firm, you realize that it is going to matter.

Tracy eventually landed at a large firm in downtown Indianapolis. The firm with which she initially started "blew up" six months after she took the job, and she was thrilled to find a job with a larger, more stable and growing firm.

She describes the culture at her firm as "incredible." Despite not considering important work-life balance issues six years ago when she joined the firm, it is the type of workplace that she would be seeking out now had she not found it sooner. Tracy felt the firm had an exciting and young vibe to it. She was actually interviewed by all women at her firm, while at another firm only men interviewed her. She felt a real connection to the firm and knew it would be a good fit.

When Tracy discovered she was pregnant, she sought guidance from two single mothers at the firm. She now serves in a mentoring role to younger associates navigating maternity leave and pregnancy issues within the firm. Tracy is also in the initial stages of developing a professional women's group through her local bar association that addresses the concerns of motherhood. She finds this particularly important because of the lack of female role models at the highest levels of the profession.

Tracy's hours are not what they were before she had a daughter. She finds this particularly troubling when she is being judged in a group, as she was in law school. Internally, she struggles because it is her inclination to be an overachiever and work hard to prove it, but she has to balance the responsibility of being a mom.

As in many firms, Tracy's firm has seen attrition of female lawyers, and it concerns both Tracy and her firm. "It is really important to younger women to have older female role models to look to"—not only from a standpoint of working mothers but also in understanding how to develop business. Tracy notes that she cultivates clients differently than men. For example, she is not particularly comfortable at this stage taking a potential male client to dinner after work in order to develop business. Having female role models to help her understand how to progress in the profession is a key to her success.

Basically, from Tracy's standpoint, if a firm is going to hire women, these female attorneys need to know that there are women they can rely on for advice and counsel. The ultimate question in finding the right workplace might be "Is there a place for me, and how do I go about finding it?" Her firm is very flexible and treats attorneys "like adults." Tracy had twelve weeks of paid maternity leave but does not have set vacation or sick time. She has billable hours that she needs to meet, but can adapt her schedule to her life as warranted. She leaves the office by 5:30 p.m. four days a week and stays late one evening. If her daughter is sick, she does not need to ask anyone for permission to stay at home or work from home, but she needs to cover her clients and make her billable hours.

In Tracy's opinion, the law is a very hard career for a mom. The profession needs to change because the way that attorneys are judged and valued is really tough on women:

> I think that women lose credit for origination sometimes. I don't think that firms realize the role that women play within things. Or they don't get brought into stuff as much because the firm fears their child commitments. I think sometimes we get excluded because they want to be mindful of our commitments, but they don't even ask us because they are trying to be almost chivalrous and say, "Well, you have to go home, I don't want to burden you with this." So I think it is a difficult career because you are working in a career that ultimately does not value your personal time, no matter what. And also so ingrained with this is that there is not a woman at the top making these decisions. There are not a lot of women identifying—"Hey, this is how we can still be a great firm but make this a better place for women." We don't have women on our executive committees, our review committees, or our compensation committees saying we could still do this another way and get better results for some of the people. Men don't identify our issues. They just don't. They don't get it and they don't see it.

When she came back from work after maternity leave, a partner called her on a Friday when she happened to be out of the office. He said to her, "I am so sorry, Tracy. I didn't realize Friday was your 'mommy day.'" She had to remind him that she did work full time. Sometimes it feels like she is always overcoming hurdles and assumptions. Although she thinks that most people are simply trying to be nice, she does feel that she has to fight against being excluded.

Tracy considers this especially important in the compensation structure of law firms, where clients are passed down from male partner to male partner. This composition excludes women from participating at the highest levels because they do not have access to the most coveted clients. Many law firm business development teams are made up of men. However, as women fill more in-house counsel positions, they increasingly want to see women on their team. In Tracy's opinion, firms that don't take that seriously are going to lose business.

As women advance, she hopes to break through the assumptions that she encounters:

> Looking at people as more than a commodity . . . valuing them for what they actually bring to the table . . . making sure that everything is not just driven on metrics but also quality and what somebody brings to the law firm [is important]. Because if you don't have people of different backgrounds or genders, you are going to miss out on a perspective, and that is going to matter to some client at some point to have that perspective, and the firm has to be willing to embrace that.

One of the ways that Tracy has combated the law firm business development model is through her participation in the local Democratic Party. When she was pregnant with her daughter, she ran eight campaigns for Democratic judges, which required ten to twenty hours of unbillable time per week. Her firm supported this endeavor because it gave her credibility with the judges whom she also came to know well. Tracy makes it clear that the judges were not more likely to rule in her favor; however, they knew she was a hard worker, and it helped her overcome stereotypes of being a young female attorney. Her service to the party also gave her access to people in positions of power as a young attorney. She made important connections, and it allowed her to explore her passion for politics. Incidentally, the feminist in her loved showing what she could do while pregnant.

> Advice: Pursue your passions and find a way to relate them to your work.

Just four months pregnant this time around, Tracy has made the decision to delay telling her firm about her pregnancy for as long as possible. She particularly does not want to be passed over for choice projects because she is expecting. Tracy considers being pregnant at work more difficult than being a mother because people within the legal profession see her differently as a pregnant woman. She has a reputation for being tough and did not like how pregnancy made people look at her as if she was "softer." In addition, it seemed as if everyone wanted to discuss her pregnancy. Essentially, she felt as if she could no longer be in the "guys club"—playing fantasy football and drinking beer. Her pregnancy made it evident she was different. It is frustrating to her because she wants her identity at work to be "tough litigator" first and foremost, not "mommy."

Tracy is clearly excelling in what she might consider a male world at this point, despite the fact that nearly 50 percent of law students are women. The attrition of female attorneys within the profession troubles her as she knocks on the door for partnership. Colleagues who have left her firm or are at other large firms and may be considering leaving have confided to Tracy that sometimes they feel that they "just can't hack it," and it has been a difficult realization. Tracy wants to prove that she can achieve her definition of success within the profession, despite shifting priorities.

On the other hand, Tracy loves being a mom, and her excitement at having another child is evident. She remarks, "It gives you a reason to be your best, and you want to help somebody else become this whole person. . . . I love teaching her, and I love watching her learn." She and her husband enjoy watching their daughter develop. Being a mom gives Tracy a reason to drop all of the seriousness and ambition she brings to work and be a kid again. She loves doing crafts, coloring, and playing with her daughter. It gives her a sense of reliving her own childhood, but, in her words, "It's even better because you are sharing it with someone who means everything to you."

Sometimes Tracy feels like she is shortchanging her daughter when she gets home from work and does not feel like engaging. After giving all her energy at the office, it can be hard to get into "mommy mode." Her daughter wants to play outside, and Tracy feels like sitting on the couch and popping in a DVD. She has to remind herself that being with her daughter is the best time of her day and enjoy it.

Tracy also feels that she brings her work stress home, more than her laid-back husband does. She sometimes deals with what might be termed "mommy guilt" when her daughter calls for her husband instead of her. She also feels badly if she doesn't see her daughter for a whole day because of work, leaving before her daughter wakes up and arriving home after she is asleep. Overall, Tracy does not believe her career affects her daughter negatively. She sees her daughter play "going to work" where she packs her bags and pretends to leave, but says, "Then I am going home to take care of my kids."

In the future as her daughter attends school, Tracy foresees that many of her daughter's peers will have stay-at-home moms. She worries about being the mom who misses events, brings the store-bought cookies to school, or doesn't decorate the house for holidays. Tracy wonders if her daughter is missing out on something because of her choice to pursue a career. Because of these concerns, Tracy focuses on the experiences that she thinks are most important and tries to let the rest go.

> Advice: Choose the things that are most important and let the rest go.

Tracy hopes that her daughter can see her in court one day. She feels that ultimately her daughter will be glad that both of her parents worked. She also thinks her daughter will want to work because she is interested in so many things. However, Tracy does not necessarily want to pressure her daughter to be a lawyer, because she feels that it may limit her own interests. As both Tracy and her husband are attorneys, as well as many members of their extended family, Tracy hopes that her daughter will feel the freedom to explore other avenues. However, Tracy describes her daughter as a very verbal and outgoing child, so perhaps it runs in the family.

As with many working moms, Tracy's biggest challenge is finding time for herself. She is always on someone else's schedule, whether it is the firm, her clients', or her daughter's. She feels that she has lost a sense of some of the things she used to care about—taking care of herself by working out or reading. In addition, friendships and relationships change once children enter the picture. There is just not as much time to devote to others. This lack of quality time has been a new frontier.

Tracy admitted that sometimes this lack of "me time" has boiled over to misplaced anger at other people, including her husband, with whom she shares a generally supportive relationship. However, she has found it hard not to feel anger or resentment when trying to juggle two full-time careers.

She has also tried to be mindful of being a good wife. Tracy and her husband, Travis, have a strong partnership. They have both made sacrifices so that their family takes precedence, especially on the weekends. While other fathers might be golfing or at football games, Travis spends his weekends with their daughter at Gymboree, soccer practice, and swimming lessons. By reinforcing this family bond, it is clear that they are in it together and make decisions with their family as the priority.

However, negotiating work-life issues has had its ups and downs. Her husband was a public defender for six years, eventually becoming the supervisor of the misdemeanor division. He now works as the Executive Director of an Arrestee Processing Center, which operates twenty-four hours a day, seven days a week. He works six days a week, sometimes during third shift in the evenings.

When both parents have demanding jobs, often one career has to take precedence. Tracy and Travis have needed to address this issue. Tracy is considered breadwinner of the family. Her husband's work as a public servant is important to both of them, but unless they want to change their lifestyle, her job technically has to pay their bills.

About a month after returning to work from maternity leave, Tracy and Travis found themselves in a new situation. He was used to her doing everything for their daughter, as she did during her maternity leave. However, now back at work, she needed to perform and ramp up her hours. Essentially, because he was leaving the house before 8:00 a.m. and returning after 6:00 p.m., Tracy was able to work only from 9:00 a.m. until 5:00 p.m. in order to relieve the nanny. These kinds of hours were unacceptable for her to continue to perform at the level she needed to advance at the firm. Tracy and Travis needed to negotiate who would go in early and who would stay late at work to balance both of their work obligations.

Their discussion boiled over into an argument about career priorities and salary. Tracy laid it on the line, saying, "If we really are getting down to it, my career has to come first, unless you want to change our lifestyle. I cannot keep my job and go in these hours." Although this is a tough issue to confront, many couples address salary and responsibility imbalances. In fact, when Tracy and Travis discussed the possibility of having him be a stay-at-home dad, one of the factors in the equation was that Tracy felt she might resent him. If he took her daughter to the zoo while Tracy spent the day working, she did not think it would be good for their relationship, and eventually it would be harder for him to get back into the legal field.

In navigating various work issues, one bright light for Tracy and her family was finding their nanny. When she began her search for child-care, Tracy was concerned about the cost of a nanny, and she wasn't sure how to go about finding one. Therefore, originally she decided to send her daughter to a daycare close to her downtown office. However, with a week left in her maternity leave, she and her daughter visited the day-care, and the reality of the situation hit Tracy hard. She made the decision that she did not want to have her daughter in a daycare, but in her home. With only a few days to find someone, she broke down . . . and was rescued from her despair from an unlikely source.

> Advice: Let people in your life know your needs!

It happened on that particular day that Tracy visited the daycare, her regular cleaning person was not available and sent a substitute. When Tracy arrived home, they chatted and played with the baby together. The woman asked her what her plans were for childcare, and Tracy explained her dilemma—they were signed up for a daycare, but she was having second thoughts. On the spot, the woman volunteered to be their nanny. Even better, they knew mutual people and her husband was a police officer. Tracy felt comfortable, and they worked out an arrangement.

> Advice: Leaving childcare decisions until the week before you go back to work usually is not a good idea, but sometimes it works.

Her nanny is ultimately the glue that makes her life work. She is both dependable and flexible and helps out with laundry and cleaning the house. She is also a kind and trustworthy person that they feel no reservations about having in their home with their daughter. Having her childcare situation settled seems to have made it easier for Tracy to welcome a second child; however, she had reservations initially.

Tracy was worried particularly about being on maternity leave the year before she would be considered for partner because she thought it might hurt her chances. She considered trying for a second child a year earlier but then decided that it would be better for their family to wait. She realized that this was a decision she had to make based on her family, rather than her career. She hopes that the firm will see her potential and that she can meet their expectations but describes partnership as a "moving target" right now.

Her ultimate career goal is to make partner and be a respected female attorney. She wants to break barriers and have a reputation as a fierce litigator. She knows she will have to make sacrifices to get there and that her children must come first. In her words, "If that means that I am not the first person in line here to be the big shot superstar, then that suffers, but I am not going to give up my kids."

When asked what advice she would give to other women practicing at large firms and contemplating having a family, she responds, "You need a supportive partner." A woman has to have the desire to have both a thriving career and a family so that she will organize her life to make it work. She believes that the support of her husband has been a key to her success. He is a true partner. She remarks, "I don't think I would have been able to get as far as I have in six years if I didn't have somebody who was there supporting me and helping me when I couldn't do it myself." In Tracy's opinion a woman can practice law and be a mother, but in order to be at a larger firm, a support system has to be in place so that a woman can focus on her career instead of stressing out about her responsibilities as a mother.

> Advice: Cultivate a support system.

In the long run, Tracy believes that being a mom has made her a more practical and realistic lawyer, with both her own time and her legal strategy as applied to clients. She recalls something that a mentor once told her:

If you go for capitalism without a heart, you will ultimately fail every time because the only way capitalism works in a society is if people remember that we are all people and we all have to somehow find a way to work together. I think that is something you can bring to the table as a parent by reminding everybody that this isn't just business, these are people; we are all people, and we have to remember to put that sensitivity in there. We need to treat people respectfully. We need to always remember that the ultimate goal is working for the greater good, instead of [the idea that] "we are all businesses and out to screw everybody for money." I think that is something that easily gets lost in our profession. . . . I think that it is something that women possibly remember more than men.

POSTSCRIPT:
Tracy followed up with this e-mail several months later:

I ended up having quite an extraordinary experience with my pregnancy and my experience with the firm and thought you might find it interesting. The short version is I was diagnosed with a potentially life-threatening condition during pregnancy that required strict bed rest at thirty-one weeks and eventual hospitalization at thirty-four weeks. Despite my condition, I was mentally able to work and my firm allowed me to work from home (and hospital) for almost seven weeks and did not require me to go on disability or FMLA. I billed almost my full requirement and then delivered a healthy baby girl three weeks early.

Chapter Two

LARGE FIRM BEST PRACTICES

*"I can live with some regrets about opportunities
not taken in my career.
I can't live with regrets about time I didn't spend
with my children."*
—Elizabeth McBride

ALTHOUGH SHE TRIED TO POSTPONE A CAREER in the law by delaying law school for three years, Elizabeth McBride ultimately decided to become an attorney, following both her mother and sister into the profession. Despite wanting to try another career path, Elizabeth credits her mother's influence with helping her choose a legal career.

I could not deny that she shaped my decision and influenced me to go to law school. My mom was a single mom, and it was a career that gave her the ability to financially support two daughters on her own, and it was one in which she earned respect from her peers. I certainly saw that growing up. I think whether conscious or not, it did affect my decision to become a lawyer.

Elizabeth was born and raised in San Francisco. She attended Princeton University, studying Politics. She graduated first in her department and summa cum laude. After graduation, she took a position in Washington, DC, at The Urban Institute, an economic and social policy research think tank. Elizabeth worked in their Justice Policy Center for three years, working on prisoner reentry and incarceration and its effects on children and families. After three years at The Urban Institute, she headed back to the Bay area, choosing Stanford Law School.

Early in her career, before she even headed to law school, a "phenomenal" mentor who encouraged her to invest in her personal life as well as her career influenced Elizabeth. She gave Elizabeth these words of wisdom: "Women in life have a short window in which to find a partner and have children, you have your entire life to have a career." With that advice, Elizabeth happily met and married her husband prior to law school.

> Advice: The right time to have a child is when it is right for you.

During her first year, another student at Stanford approached Elizabeth, asking her if she had considered starting a family in law school. She encouraged Elizabeth to think about it and speak with women lawyers with families. She spoke with two or three lawyers who not only encouraged her to start a family while in law school but also expressed regret at not having done so themselves. They indicated that they had more time in school to juggle a family, and she would have a year or two of being a mom under her belt before embarking on a full-time career.

With that in mind, she became pregnant during her second year of law school and interviewed in the fall of her second year for a summer associate job. Being pregnant, she asked very different questions than she might have otherwise. After receiving offers, Elizabeth honed in on meeting with women at the firms about their experiences. She had not yet divulged that she was pregnant, but she wanted to know what to expect after she was done expecting. The firm she chose was "clearly, categorically above the rest, having reached a critical mass of women who were mothers and working." The firm was large and currently has over 1,000 attorneys working in 23 offices. To Elizabeth, it may not have been as well known as some of the firms chosen by her Stanford classmates, but without a doubt, it had the happiest working moms.

Elizabeth's first years at the firm were punctuated by the births of her three children. She started her summer associate position when she was nine months pregnant. Two weeks later she welcomed a baby daughter, taking six weeks off. She then finished out the final three to four weeks of the summer, and ultimately received an offer. After her third year of law school and taking the bar exam, she became pregnant and had her second daughter midway through her first year as an associate. She had her third daughter at the beginning of her third year as an associate.

She attributes her ability to balance her career and family to the support of her law firm. Elizabeth credits an incredible managing partner with personal experience related to the legal mom dilemma. His wife had been an attorney at another large law firm. She ultimately chose to leave the firm because she felt that she was not able to balance raising three children with her career. Elizabeth comments, "As a result of that personal experience, he was incredibly sensitive to wanting women to succeed. Where he saw his wife lack choices in her pathways to success at big law, he wanted to create avenues for women to succeed."

In negotiating, Elizabeth always framed her bargaining points as good things for the firm as well as for her. She articulated up front that her career as a first-year associate was not going to mirror what her peers were doing. As she pursued such negotiations, she was careful to hone in on the support from the ultimate decision makers concerning her career. The message and support needed to come from the top down. The managing partner called her personally on the phone and recognized that not all career trajectories were going to be the same. She notes, "The firm has always kept their word." In the interviewing process, it was her experience that firms were very interested in expanding their cohort of working moms, and having women come into the firm who already had children and wanted careers in big law was one way to do so.

Advice: Research law firm policies and realities before taking a job.

Critical to her success at the firm was that they already had programs for working moms in place. This saved Elizabeth from having to ask for accommodations or to risk being stigmatized as a working mom. "Seeing that women were already taking advantage of them—and especially more senior associates in the firm—it was just a no brainer for me that it was the right place for me."

The three programs for legal moms included the following:

- An outstanding maternity leave policy—18 weeks of paid leave at full salary. Attorneys could take up to six months with complete continuation of full benefits. This program allowed legal moms to resume working when they were ready, rather than rush women who were not emotionally or physically ready to come back.
- Alternative work arrangements—This program was available to both women and men. An attorney could work any percentage of time down to 70 percent, with full benefits; however, salary and billable requirements were prorated. Attorneys in this program were able to stay on partnership track the entire time. It essentially gave working parents flexibility and the ability to work on fewer matters. Partners who acted as mentors could intervene in situations where those in the firm were not respecting the part-time arrangement. Also, a partner in charge of the whole program performed quarterly check-ins with participants. From Elizabeth's perspective, this program made "really great business sense."
- On ramping—This program allowed a legal mom to return to work at 60 percent and increase work time until the baby's first birthday. At that point, the attorney could decide whether to work full time or formally choose to participate in the alternative work arrangement program.

The firm continued to promote Elizabeth, but she was also proactive when she came back from each maternity leave to seek opportunities that she needed to develop as an attorney, whether it was deposition experience or oral argument experience. As she has primarily worked in the area of intellectual property litigation, the firm made an effort to keep her going on track. Despite her absences from the office, her star was never tarnished. Elizabeth comments:

> The stigma factor comes in when you don't have a critical mass of people participating in these kinds of programs. If you become the outlier, then it is easy to be marginalized because no one is looking

out for you. There is no sort of firm-wide commitment or policy that "we want to make this work." That is just not the case at my firm. From the top down, they want to make it work. They have made it easy for partners to help associates, and also easy for associates to advocate for themselves. To some extent, it does require a lot of really good management of your career.

Perhaps this firm is an anomaly in the legal profession, but Elizabeth does see many of her colleagues at the firm balancing family and work successfully and believes that they are great role models for her. "My hope is to continue to do it and carve out paths for other women."

Elizabeth also is careful about setting realistic expectations. She is clear to project her commitment to the firm; however, she is keenly aware of her own priorities.

No one else knows what your obligations are at home. It's quite frankly not their job to know. Only you know what obligations you have at home that you have to meet. Instead of sitting quietly and stressing about it in a conference . . . what has certainly worked for me, up front saying these are the hours that I am unavailable, other than that you can count on me.

Elizabeth carves out time between 5:00 p.m. and 8:00 p.m. as family time. She can fire up her laptop after the kids are in bed, but reserves early evening hours to focus on her children and husband. When necessary, a partner has assisted in drawing boundaries with clients, letting them know that Elizabeth is extremely responsive but that she is not available in the early evening hours. Part of her deal is that she is compensated less so that she doesn't have to be available during those hours.

Elizabeth also takes it upon herself to schedule meetings when opportunities arise in order to control the timing of meetings. By doing this seemingly administrative task, she can optimize her schedule.

She has learned how to respectfully and tactfully decline assignments when she is unable to take on a new project, an important skill for all associates. Elizabeth is careful not to give a particular reason.

If I have to say "no" to an assignment, even if I know it is because I have these other deadlines and I need to be home by [a certain] time. I don't give a reason. I just say, "No, I am really sorry I can't take that.

If another opportunity comes up, I hope you keep me in mind." Or if someone needs to set a meeting at 5:30, I say, "Can we do it at 4:00?"

Elizabeth notes that women are afraid to be expendable to their firms in this economy. If a woman is unavailable for a particular assignment, she may find her career stifled. On the contrary, Elizabeth sees some value in the fact that someone else can jump in and assist if there is a family emergency. In her opinion, this should not devalue one's contribution to the firm, client, matter, or assignment. "We need to dispel the notion that we are all important, all the time." By working in a team environment, Elizabeth has been able to make her absences from the office for maternity leaves seamless. This type of arrangement is in the best interests of the client.

Currently, Elizabeth is on maternity leave with her third child; however, most recently she utilized the firm's alternative work arrangement program, working at 85 percent. She has employed different childcare strategies since she had her first daughter in law school. Initially, she did a nanny-share with a friend who had a child around the same time. After law school, when she went to work at the firm, she employed a full-time nanny. At this point, her older two children attend a daycare/preschool, and she will utilize a nanny-share again with her third child. As Elizabeth describes it, she pays an "obscene" amount for childcare, but she sees it as an investment in her career. She heeds the advice her mom gave her: "You can only have a career if you feel really good about the childcare you have."

Elizabeth has been careful to be clear about her own priorities. In her words, "Only one thing gets to come first." This means that her actions must live out her priorities. In her case, her children are her priority. She may have passed on opportunities that would have advanced her career, but she has made such sacrifices consciously. She has had to say, "Not now, maybe later."

Although her children are her first priority, she states that she never feels "mom guilt" about working. She attributes this in part to the fact that her mother worked as an attorney and did a wonderful job of putting her children first. Elizabeth also indicates that having had sixteen months with her oldest daughter before she began her career as an associate gave her time to figure out her own brand of motherhood. She comments, "The hardest thing about maternity leave is the anxiety about going back to work." For Elizabeth, the benefit of having a longer maternity leave with each child has been the ability to emotionally process the kind of mother that she is.

> I believe in my heart of hearts that I am a better mom because I have a career. I love the intellectual stimulation. I enjoy being around other adults during the day. I love being able to go to the bathroom when I want and eat lunch when I want and put on a suit or a little makeup. I really love it. I love coming home and making dinner and hearing about my kids' days. I know that they have had great days.

Elizabeth does have moments where she feels sad because she misses something at her daughters' school, but she reminds herself that the feeling is hers and that her daughters are fine. They may not necessarily even remember. She remarks, "As mothers, we torture ourselves, about the little things we missed or the time we might have been late. They just need to know that you love them."

When Elizabeth first started working, she and her husband sat down and talked about how they were going to make things work. She describes their arrangement in caring for their children as 50/50. The fact that she has a career allows him to have a career that he enjoys, but he does not have to work insane hours because she is also a breadwinner for the family. Elizabeth loves that he can also share in the childcare and that he has a great relationship with their daughters. As an engineer, his schedule is flexible and predictable. They found that her afternoons are less predictable, so he covers the afternoons while she gets the kids ready in the mornings. They have both made compromises in their careers so that they can be the parents they want to be.

Despite her terrific work environment, Elizabeth still has times where she feels overwhelmed. She has learned to live on "a lot less sleep and a lot more Starbucks."

> I wake up feeling good because I feel good about what I can control. I've worked a lot on accepting that there are things that I can't control in life. That's parenting. . . .

In her opinion, it is a matter of knowing what is important to you and finding a job that has the top three things that are important and living with the rest.

At this point, Elizabeth has not known any female lawyers who have left the profession after having children; however, she acknowledges the issue that some women choose to stay home because some firms are less than accommodating. In her opinion, if firms gave women a year to come back (not entirely paid), more women would return to work. Elizabeth comments that having a first child is "life altering and universe shifting."

> It takes a lot of time to sort out what you want, for you, for your child, for your family unit, and for your career. To have to make that decision when you have a really small infant, I think is almost impossible. The deck is stacked against going back to a big law position.

Women may also fail to advocate for extended maternity leave or a part-time return. Elizabeth encourages women to ask the question, "Is there a model that might work for me?"—whether it is six months off or reduced billable hour requirements. Rather than try to maintain the standard of pre-baby work and ultimately leaving the workplace, women need to "reconceptualize" the lawyers they are going to be once they have children.

From a firm's perspective, Elizabeth notes that it makes business sense for firms to work to retain intelligent legal moms. She comments, "There is no more efficient worker than a working mom." Working moms have a huge incentive to manage their time, be organized, and produce a high-quality work product. She also notes that many women on part-time schedules still end up billing more than their part-time arrangement.

> At the end of the day, it is more cost effective for the firm to let you take three months more unpaid and have you come back and resume your client relationships and pick up where you left off, than the cost of them going out and trying to hire someone else, train them, get them up to speed, and develop those client relationships. Advocate for what you want.

Advice: Negotiate with the firm's interests in mind.

Elizabeth advises that whenever women plan to ask for accommodations to keep in mind that law firms/companies are about their bottom line; therefore, women need to think about what they want and how such a request could benefit the firm, either in dollars or nonmonetary assets, such as client relationships or recruiting.

> How can I translate this into something that works for the firm and for me? . . . You will have more receptive ears if you are thinking about the firm's interest as well. At the end of the day, they are a business and they are there to make money and service their clients. You have a lot to offer, but you have to think about it in terms of their business model.

As Elizabeth's mother was also an attorney, she is able to contrast her own career and the expanded opportunities available now for women. Her mom marvels that Elizabeth is at a large law firm. "Big law was not an option for women who didn't want to play the boys' game with the boys." Her mother made the choice to go into the public sector. She was the first woman to return after maternity leave and the first woman to carve out a part-time schedule. Her mother loved her "flourishing" career. "She knew what she wanted and she lived it every day." Her mother is amazed at the opportunities that Elizabeth has, because there was a time when you could not "have it all."

As a child, Elizabeth never once felt like she was shortchanged by her mother's career. Therefore, Elizabeth doesn't second guess whether she is sacrificing too much to her own career while raising her children. Her mother's success at juggling career and family allowed Elizabeth to rid herself of the mommy guilt with which so many women struggle.

> It's okay if your kids are not enough. I [am] not saying that your kids are not amazing and wonderful and the most important things in your life. But it is okay to want more. It is okay to find an intellectually challenging career that is really wonderful. And to want that in order to feel fulfilled. You can still be a great mom and want that.

Her mom has been pivotal in Elizabeth's adult life in giving her guidance on topics like graduate school, performance evaluations, finding mentors, managing client relationships, and figuring out her career.

> I am so grateful to her for sticking it out in a workforce that wasn't as friendly to women, and I feel like I owe that to my daughters to try to make it even better for them if this is the career they want to pursue or any career they want to pursue. I hope that I am helping to make their paths that much better.

Elizabeth remarks that it is very difficult for women who want a family to make choices about the trajectory of their careers until they have had their first child because they don't know yet how they might be affected by parenthood. She also has noticed how advice from an earlier generation may not always fit current circumstances. A lawyer mom, saying, "this is what worked for me, so this is how you should do it" may not work, because every situation is different. Elizabeth would love to see women in her generation be able to have choices and show other women that they can carve their own path. She absolutely credits those women who have gone before her and blazed trails, but women can also pave their own way.

Maybe it is because I have three girls and I want to set a good example for them. I want to show them that you can be happy and fulfilled in your personal life and be great with your family and take vacations and have wonderful family dinners every night, but also it is okay for mom to get up and do something important and great.

As she continues to carve out her own path, Elizabeth feels that she is making a strong contribution that is valued by her firm, people are rooting for her, and she enjoys her work. Most importantly, she has the tools that will allow her to succeed at work and at home.

Chapter Three

THE BIG APPLE
LEGAL MOM

*"You are committed to your job. You are committed
to your family, and you just get things done."*
—Dyan Finguerra-DuCharme

DYAN FINGUERRA-DUCHARME FELT THAT LAW was her destiny since the time she was a child. She was always arguing with her parents about fairness. In middle school, a close friend was ill and missed a test. She was not given the same instructions the following day when she took the test. Dyan took on her friend's case, arguing with the teacher over the fairness of the situation. She was summarily sent to the principal. Dyan remembers,

> The teacher told me, "You need to stop being the country lawyer." I think that it sort of implanted in my mind the idea that I had a calling to be a lawyer and to be always arguing about what was fair and what was equal.

As an adult, Dyan pursued her passion for fairness as a lawyer with a career at two large firms in New York City. As an undergraduate at Hamilton College in Clinton, New York, Dyan majored in Government. She spent a summer as an intern for Congresswoman Patricia Schroeder. After college, Dyan took a year off because she had not done very well on her LSAT. She took a job as a legal assistant, retook the LSAT and scored well. She was accepted at Brooklyn Law School, where she went on to graduate with distinctions in several subject areas.

Dyan's winning personality and love of cheesecake were what eventually led her to a job at one of the country's largest law firms, which will be referred to as "Firm A" throughout this chapter. As a third-year student, Dyan was scheduled for an interview with Firm A. She was excited but knew it was a long shot. She received a call from career services that the interviewer was running early and would she mind coming in a few minutes ahead of schedule. Dyan promptly went to the interview, walking in as the attorney was about to bite into a piece of Junior's cheesecake. Dyan apologized for interrupting his lunch, to which he slid the cheesecake aside. She protested, asking if he had ever had Junior's cheesecake. She insisted he eat the cheesecake, and he invited her to have a slice as well. Essentially, they just informally talked over cheesecake. She doesn't even remember if he asked her a real interview question. She was surprised to receive a callback interview. She was even more surprised, as was Brooklyn Law School, when she received a job offer. It is very clear that Dyan has exceptional people skills and can advocate for herself.

She went to Firm A immediately after law school, hoping to practice Intellectual Property Law, to which she had been introduced as a summer associate at a Philadelphia law firm. Unfortunately, she fell into the Antitrust Law group. Dyan describes it as a great group of people, but not the law she wanted to practice. She decided to apply for a judicial clerkship, and a magistrate judge in Brooklyn hired her. She describes her experience as "wonderful, incredible."

After her clerkship, Dyan had multiple offers. She came back to Firm A under the condition that she could work on Intellectual Property Law, specifically trademarks. It was very good timing, as some pharmaceutical cases were heating up. The trademark partner needed help and welcomed her into the group.

Within a couple of years, the same partner had an opportunity to join a growing New York office of a large firm, which shall be identified as "Firm B" in this chapter. Dyan made the decision to go with the partner to Firm B, as he was her mentor and she knew her best chance of making partner at either firm hinged on his retirement. Knowing that the possibility of partnership was still a few years away, Dyan and her husband made the decision to start thinking about having children:

> I never wanted to be one of those women that didn't start to have kids until I was a partner. I kind of knew that was not feasible and that being a partner is more demanding than being an associate. I thought it would be better if I had young children when I became partner rather than having newborn babies.

With this in mind, Dyan welcomed her first daughter in 2001 and her second daughter in 2003. Meanwhile, her mentor made the decision to continue working past age sixty-five. As Dyan had somewhat based her life plan on his retirement age and her hopeful ascension into his partnership slot, she was in a quandary. Their practice at Firm B was growing but did not yet justify having two trademark partners in the New York office.

When Dyan had her first child, she was officially a fifth-year associate and was approaching partnership level. Partnership was still the brass ring. Dyan explains, "It was important. . . . I always knew that any hope that any chance I had of partnership was tied to [the partner's] retirement."

Since partnership was off the table for the time being, Dyan decided to work part time after having her second child, having worked from home one day a week after her first daughter was born. However, she was still deeply committed to her work despite her part-time status:

> I was always dedicated completely to the firm. I think it is a real misnomer that people think that once you start having babies your dedication to the firm lessens at all. It really doesn't. In fact, I think that actually sometimes your children's perception is that you have more of a dedication to the firm than you do to them because you are constantly on the blackberry and you are constantly telling them to be quiet because you are on the phone for work or you've got to log in for ten minutes to do work. I think from their perception your dedication is more to the firm than it is to them. I guess it is more like when you get on that treadmill at high speed as a fifth through eighth year [associate] . . . at that point for me, I was able to see the big picture and to recognize that my elevation was not going to happen until [my mentor] was a year from retirement.

Dyan had her third child in 2007 and made the decision to return to the office on a full-time basis. As she was very senior within the firm at that point, her hours were manageable, and the practice of law had changed to accommodate more remote work arrangements, such as logging into the law firm system from home.

Dyan believes that Firm B had great maternity policies. She was allowed three months paid leave and could take as much time as she wanted unpaid. She also generally found the firm to be a good working environment, commenting, "I honestly did not witness any discrimination based on the fact that women had children." Dyan was relatively open about her status as a mother and did not necessarily worry that it was hindering her career.

Despite the generally positive environment, Dyan did have some concerns. It bothered her that the firm would call women after they came back from maternity leave and would suggest that they push back partnership consideration by a year. Their reasoning followed along the lines of "Oh, it gives you a better runway, gives you more time to ramp back up. There is always a ramp down before you go out on leave and a ramp up process when you come back." In Dyan's opinion, "It really was insane. It was crazy that they said that to women who came back from maternity leave."

Dyan knew of one particular woman who billed 300 hours in her first month back after maternity leave. She was stuck on a case in California and ended up pumping milk and express mailing it back to her husband in New York. This type of dedication to career should not have been penalized by delaying her chances at partnership by one year.

In the span of a career, four months of leave is nothing in Dyan's opinion. In comparing what her peers might have done in such a time span, she remarks, "When you are at that level, one more deposition is not going to make you more qualified to make partner."

Dyan also felt that Firm B did not always make clear the ramifications of maternity leave for each attorney. Dyan had her third child in May and returned to work right after Labor Day. Because she was so senior within the firm, there was a ramp-up period as she acclimated to client matters and built back up her business. During this time her hours weren't great, but her record at the firm was good, and she was never told to be concerned. At the end of the year, she learned that she was not going to get a bonus. For the first five months of the year, she was billing exceptional hours and felt that her time should at least have been prorated to give her some bonus. In fact, she could have hunted around for more work when she returned in the form of document reviews or other routine matters, but she was more concerned with her own practice area. In her words, "Nobody was looking out for me." Dyan felt that fair warning should have been given.

During her time at Firm B, Dyan feels that she worked with great people; however, like many associates, she had her occasional problems with a difficult partner questioning her work ethic. One particular day, he said to her, "You think you work hard; you don't work hard." This comment really stuck with Dyan. At the time, she had a three year old and a one year old. She was up half the night nursing, putting in more hours at work than her part-time schedule required, and logging back into the system every evening after she put her kids to bed. Dyan comments, "To say that I didn't work hard was such a blow to my psyche, because at the time all I was doing was working." This particular partner did not have children and had no understanding of what her life was really like. Regardless, she took his words to heart.

After three more years at Firm B, Dyan was at another crossroads. Partnership was still not within reach, but Dyan was on track to make Special Counsel, recognition that the type of law she did was important to the firm. Firm B was an up or out firm. Once allowed to pursue partnership, Dyan would have two chances to go for it, but if unsuccessful, would be out. In her case, the lack of partnership did not necessarily relate to motherhood, but to her practice area. Her practice area took a blow when one of their most important clients had not chosen Firm B as a preferred law firm. Some of the work that Dyan so enjoyed would soon be leaving the firm. She and another colleague made the decision to leave Firm B and follow the client, ironically back to Firm A, where Dyan had originally started her career. In May of 2010, after 10 years at Firm B, Dyan made the move:

> I was ready to move on. The firm was not telling me to leave at all. They were shocked and surprised when I did leave. So I wasn't given any message to go. I had been at the firm for so long and had been through a merger. I was the first person there to have a baby and start a family. I was very involved with women's issues and work-life balance issues. I think they were kind of shocked that I was just leaving. Sometimes you have these moments in life where an opportunity

knocks and you really can't turn it down. It was a total risk because I had a very nice and comfortable life there, and I liked the people who I worked with. But I kind of wanted to go somewhere where they were really going to invest in me, and I think that I had been at [Firm B] for too long. They had already decided that they were not going to make me partner, so they were not really investing in me anymore as growing and helping me grow a practice. For me, it was a great opportunity to have people look at me and see potential.

In joining Firm A as Counsel, Dyan feels that they have been very supportive of the growth of her practice. They have given her a lot of autonomy and support. At this point, her hours aren't great, but they are looking at her as a long-term investment. Firm A is telling her to "be patient" and work on building a client base. Dyan is enjoying the work and the support immensely.

As she reflects on her career at two large New York City law firms, Dyan thinks that firms have come a long way in their policies since she was a legal assistant and saw a female attorney reprimanded for wearing a pantsuit. She sees many benefits to the large firms, noting, "Things have changed so much." Both Firm A and B made it easy for her to work from home. One firm was heavily involved in cross-staffing cases with teams of people who worked all over the country. From Dyan's perspective, it didn't matter if you weren't there for "facetime" at the office because meetings were done by conference call. She relates, "The policies are becoming a lot more flexible." Using her laptop, Dyan can move her desk anywhere, especially since she has the ability to log into the system from her home office. Dyan's computer even has a headset where she can call or answer the phone as if she is at her desk:

> Firms have taken really innovative approaches. At the end of the day, if you get your work done and you do a good job, I think they don't care where the heck you did it.

Moreover, both law firms have back-up childcare policies in place to help when her kids were sick or her original care provider was unable to work. This back-up policy provides up to eighty hours of help per year. Essentially, screened babysitters can come to Dyan's home and the cost is partially subsidized by the firm. This allowed Dyan to work from home when her kids were sick, but have someone else there to entertain them. She also had the option of dropping off her children at certain daycare centers and was able to take advantage of this service when travelling to a deposition in New Jersey.

Dyan further credits the firms where she has worked with making it possible for her to manage both her work and home lives:

> I think that it is a real testament to the firms that I have worked at. Because I really do think that both firms make it so that it is possible to do if you really do love your job and the work you are doing. You can have it all. I don't think that can be said for every place.

Although the firm policies have been helpful, Dyan was also very conscious before she had children how she would manage her career and family life. Dyan cautions other women not to plan children around their career because jobs can be unpredictable, and the ability to have children is not always an easy road.

> I have witnessed people who have had babies and continued to work 2700-hour years at the expense of their kids only to not make partner. And then to look back and say, "I missed the last three years of my kid's life."

Dyan credits the importance of having a good support system as one of the strategies she uses to make it all work. Dyan utilizes both primary caregivers and back-up babysitters for those moments of panic when she can't get out of a meeting. In her opinion, women can't do it without support and backup. She also notes that husbands are playing greater roles on the home front. Her husband is hands-on with the girls. Dyan also has her parents living close by. Despite having support in place, there are still days when the job gets to her:

> There have been definite periods of time when I felt like I was going to lose my sanity, and whenever things get really hard at work . . . back at my old firm, when I had those terrible experiences with that one partner. Those are the moments when I say, "What am I doing? Why am I not a stay-at-home mom? Why don't I own my bagel shop?" Just a little dream of mine.

Advice: Keep your parenting obligations to yourself, for the most part.

In October of 2011, Dyan wrote an article titled, "Full Time . . . Everything" for *New York Metro Parents Magazine* on juggling a career with motherhood. In this article, she discusses the importance of being flexible and keeping open lines of communication with your workplace, but knowing what to communicate. Dyan feels that a legal mom does not need to wear her part-time status on her sleeve or let people know about issues related to the kids. It was always the greatest compliment to her that partners didn't know that she was part time. She simply didn't advertise it.

At the same time, Dyan has never felt like she needs to hide the fact that she is a mother. She has her children's artwork up on her office wall, and her children have visited the office. Dyan is proud of her kids and her status as a mom. Dyan explains her ability to separate her two lives:

> My view is just that I don't need to explain to people why there is a competing home obligation. You are part time to all of your clients, you are part time to all of the lawyers you work for because you are not working on anything for the most part 100%. I have got four or five different cases online at any given time. I have multiple clients that I service and multiple partners that call me up. If I am not in for the day, I could just as easily have been in a deposition all day.

Dyan will talk about the kids at work but knows where to set limits and boundaries. She doesn't hide the things she does for her children, but she also doesn't use her children as an excuse. She simply doesn't explain that she needs to leave the office to relieve her sitter, because in her words, "People do react to that."

Even in the years where she was working part time, there were months when she exceeded full-time hours. One particular year, everything came to a head in May. Dyan was working part time but still billed 250 hours during the month. She comments, "I definitely did feel like I was at the end of my rope. I knew that the end would come." She balanced this demanding time by taking more time off during the summer to spend with her girls.

Dyan describes her most challenging times when work gets busy for extended periods or unexpected issues pop up, but her day-to-day life is generally manageable. In her words, "It is very easy when my life at work is steady. When there are briefs due, when I am on teams with difficult people—that is when things get challenging."

Beyond her concerns at work, Dyan is a worrier on the home front. She not only worries about her career but also her children. She worries about who will help her own girls when they grow up and have careers. This type of mental stress gets to her—simply managing her own mental capacity to do everything she needs to do. Her husband encourages her to take time for herself. She remarks, "He always recognized how important it was for me to maintain a hobby or take time for myself. . . . That really helps." At this point, Dyan is involved in a women's running group that has great camaraderie. She also thinks running has helped her to collect her thoughts and burn nervous energy.

And Dyan is a woman with a lot of energy! She notes, "I am able to just keep going. I have a lot of energy the way my mother does. For me, I can transition from work to home." It may be why she also stresses out about not doing enough, despite everything she is juggling. Like many working moms, Dyan says, "Guilt is my biggest enemy." She is a classroom mom and never misses a concert or performance for her kids, but she still worries about not doing enough. She comments, "Guilt is such a major factor. Because of the guilt, I think that I overly compensate and do too much because I feel so guilty." She spends a lot of time with her kids on the weekends and in the evenings. Dyan also has a wonderful caregiver who comes to her home when she is working. In her words, "I have come to terms with it. . . . Everybody has those days that are filled with competing obligations."

Despite the guilt, Dyan does not feel like she has sacrificed her children for her career or vice versa. She relates, "I don't think my job has ever been affected, and I don't think my kids have been affected by my job." Generally, she doesn't think in terms of "sacrifices" in regard to the competing interests work and family. As a mother and as a lawyer, Dyan simply deals with each situation as it comes:

> I think that the sacrifices are what any mother has sacrificed. The sacrifice is that you have lost your sense of personal time. You are just always reactive to your children or your job. I think as a lawyer you lose control over your time. If I get a call now that a client has been hit with a TRO, I am going to be working for the next three days on it. It is just so reactive. It is the same thing with your kids. Who wakes up today with a sniffling nose and a sore throat?

Dyan also deals with a different type of stress living near and working in the largest city in the United States. Despite the commute and pressure, Dyan has thrived, although she does note that there are drawbacks:

> [New York City] is a giant fishbowl and it is so competitive. . . . It is so much about status. There are some people that are so hung on up on having the partner title . . . and people put so much weight to that.

When she is dealing with this type of stress, she thinks about her family and nonlegal friends who simply think of her as a great lawyer. She was more attuned to the partnership process at Firm B, but since returning to Firm A, she can reflect on life on the partnership treadmill, commenting,

> You have to be a really excellent attorney to make partner. . . . It is such a demanding process, and they take into account so many factors. Even if you are an excellent lawyer, it doesn't necessarily mean that you are going to make partner.

Dyan has stopped stressing about her title within the law firm, focusing on the work and the people with whom she works:

> I personally have come to terms that I don't need the title "partner" as long as I am happy with the work that I am doing and the people I work with. . . . Maybe someday I will make partner, but if I don't, it won't be the end of the world.

Advice: Reach out to friends in the legal field for support.

As she has navigated her career, Dyan has always had good friends in the legal field who were going through similar things at work. She advises women to reach out to their friends for emotional support:

> It is okay to show your vulnerability to your support network and your peers, but I would suggest not showing your vulnerability to the bosses, to the partners. There were plenty of times when I shut the door and cried in my office . . . but you try your best not to show that to the partners.

Dyan has not seen her peers or colleagues choosing to leave law practice to stay home and raise children, though she has seen women who have chosen not to reenter the legal field, but to focus on family after being downsized at firms. Having women in the field to whom she can relate has been important to her as she has made decisions throughout her career.

Advice: Don't put off children to focus only on career.

On a final note, Dyan advises young women embarking on a legal career not to sacrifice having children to their career. She is cultivating both a fulfilling career and a satisfying family life:

> Don't not have children because of your career path and timing of it. . . . Your whole worldview changes once you have these kids. Start the family. Your career will work its way out.

Chapter Four

SUPPORT FROM THE HOME FRONT AND THE SMALL-FIRM WORKPLACE

"Everyone's experience is very different, and mine has been very positive. You can very realistically do both."

—*Kristen Pursley*

KRISTEN PURSLEY GREW UP with a working mom and never questioned whether she would work when she grew up. She so strongly assumed she would pursue a career that when a high school classmate said that she wanted to be a stay-at-home mom, it actually shocked Kristen.

Initially, Kristen pursued an undergraduate degree in Biochemistry at Michigan State University. She thought she might pursue medical school or a PhD in order to teach. She wasn't quite sure what else to do with her degree, which ended up being in Environmental Biology and Zoology.

During her last year of college, Kristen got a job in a small law firm. Law school had never been on her radar because she did not like public speaking. However, she saw the kind of transactional work that the firm was doing and realized that it suited her talents and attention to detail. Upon graduation, Kristen took a job as a paralegal with a corporate legal department in Palo Alto, California, which helped solidify her decision to pursue law school.

Having been waitlisted at the Hastings Law School and not receiving an offer from University of Michigan, Kristen chose to move back to the Midwest to attend the University of Cincinnati Law School. Although her first year was incredibly stressful, she found a terrific group of women who became her lifelong friends. She was living apart from her then boyfriend (now husband) who had stayed in California.

Kristen pursued job opportunities in Cincinnati and in Michigan. Because both she and her husband were originally from Michigan, after her 2005 graduation, she took an offer with a small (nine attorney) firm in Pontiac, Michigan. The months after law school graduation were particularly stressful. Kristen got married, learned the unfortunate news that she had failed the Michigan Bar Exam, and discovered she was pregnant with her first child. To add further complications, she and her new husband were living in a friend's basement while she tried to make it as a lawyer. The firm had a system whereby Kristen took home 40 percent of whatever billings were paid, so it was quite a while before she made any hard money.

Kristen persevered. She took the bar exam for a second time the summer she had her first child. She took two months off work to spend time with her newborn and prepare for the bar exam. She was determined to pass the test the second time around but felt as if she made sacrifices in losing time with her new baby. In her words, "I feel like I missed out a little bit because my life had to be so regimented with studying."

When choosing to move back to Michigan, Kristen was conscious of her need for family support as a working mom. While growing up, Kristen's grandparents lived a few blocks away, and she spent a lot of time with them. She wanted the same types of connections for her own children. Her mother lives five minutes away, and her in-laws are only a few hours away. This has been critical for Kristen as she has pursued her career.

> The support we have in general—when I have to go out of town for work, my mother is here if we need help—[is essential]. My in-laws

are here. My sister-in-law helps. . . . I don't know how families have both parents working without this kind of family support.

> Advice: Finding a great childcare situation can alleviate a lot of stress

Kristen also has had the benefit of having her sister, who has an education degree, as her daycare provider since her children, now three and five, were infants. Having her sister involved with the boys has allowed Kristen to focus on work while at work, without concerns about how her kids are doing at home.

> It is huge that I have no concerns. I have no issues. They adore her. She is wonderful with them. She literally went to school to do this kind of thing. I often probably don't appreciate that as much as I should. I don't have that issue that people who send their children to daycares, where there is that thing in the back of your mind saying, "Is everything going okay there? Do I have anything to worry about?" I have nothing to worry about. She loves them to death. They love her to death. It is really ideal.

Kristen feels very lucky to have identified law as a career for herself, because she enjoys the work and it seems to fit how her brain works. Sometimes she wonders what it would be like to stay home, but she doesn't wrestle much with the idea because she can't afford not to work. Although she doesn't second-guess her decision to work, she still feels guilt for being away from her kids: "I feel like my kids aren't getting as much time as they could with me, and I am not getting as much time as I could with them."

She gives an example of a Mother's Day tea at her son's preschool. He was very upset when it was time for her to leave and threw an enormous sobbing fit. The teacher remarked to her, "He is sad because he never gets to see his mommy." This situation and the perception of the teacher really upset Kristen because she loves spending time with her children and didn't feel the remark was warranted.

Kristen has formed very few friendships with stay-at-home moms who seem to hang out socially. Another stay-at-home mom at the school, who had previously been an attorney, said to Kristen, "Oh, I didn't realize you were an attorney too. How do you do that? How do you possibly work and have the boys?" Kristen didn't really know how to answer the question but commented that her workplace was supportive and she has a lot of family support. At the same time, Kristen does feel conflicted about her dual role, trying to juggle everything. Like many other working moms, she knows that she can't do everything perfectly:

> I feel like I have to be kind of below average as a mother and below average at work because I just don't have time to put in what I feel I would like to put in with both of those situations. At the same time, I also feel like (and this is hard to admit) I kind of rely on it as an excuse for myself. I feel like if I am not living up to my standards at work, I have that excuse to rely on: "Oh, that is because I have so many commitments at home." And if I feel like I am not living up to my commitments to my children and not doing a good job there, I kind of make the excuse to myself, "Oh, that is because I am working." So at the same time, while I don't like the pressures that it puts on me, I think internally I use it as an excuse to feel better about the fact that I can't do either, and just say, "Well, I am doing the best that I can."

As the only female attorney in her office, Kristen has not had female mentors to look toward, although she has been working on building a mentorship network locally. She notices that she is dealing with so many different sides of life that her colleagues rely on their stay-at-home wives to manage. Taking care of the house, getting the dog to the groomer, meeting the cable guy are a just a few examples of some of the minute details that Kristen has to deal with in addition to her responsibilities at work and to the kids. She remarks on the other attorneys in the office:

> I think they kind of get it, but on a lot of levels, I don't think they can possibly imagine how constantly, constantly overwhelmed it feels to not just have the work stuff, but to have everything else that goes with it.

That being said, Kristen is the product of a working mother and watched her own mom deal with both sides of life as well. As a child, Kristen never thought there was anything else except Mom working and thinks it is likely the same for her kids. They look so forward to going to her sister's home during the week that it seems to work well.

However, like any working mom, Kristen sometimes feels like she is shortchanging her kids. There is always something she needs to be doing at work or on the home front. She comments,

We have a shortage of quality time where we can just sit, be with them, and play three hours of board games. . . . We do play, but I have so many things that I have to do around here on the weekends . . . so I don't get those extended periods where I would just get to be with them. There is always something to do.

Typically, Kristen works ten-hour days during the week and a couple hours each day during the weekend. However, she doesn't go into the office on weekends anymore. Her billable hours are reasonable at approximately 140 hours per month (1,680 per year). In her current arrangement with the firm, she still gets 40 percent of her billings, and based on her experience and knowledge, her work is highly collectable.

At this point, Kristen has not thought much about cutting back her hours or going part time. She knows how much work she needs to do to be successful and can't imagine being able to do it in less time:

It just hinders your ability to get ahead in this business. I already struggle so much with business development, and I am in there all of the time doing so much and working, working, working. Doing it part time, I just feel like it would hinder my progression.

Kristen is really happy with her situation at work and feels that the small-firm environment has been amenable to her family situation. At any point during a workday, she can leave the office to deal with family issues, and she is not punished for it or treated differently because of it. Kristen states, "Everyone is always understanding. I don't feel guilty." During the last couple of years, she needed to take her son to preschool at 9:00 a.m., arriving to the office after his drop-off. She made up the time on the other end of the day. Kristen thinks her situation in which there are no workplace hassles is rare:

This is a really unique place to be able to be a mom and to be a lawyer. Even the fact that anyone has even mentioned to me the partnership idea, I am thrilled that I can have all of this. I feel so fortunate that I found this place where I can do this. At big firms, no one is going to be cushy and touchy-feely about your commitments at home generally . . . there are not a lot of people going out of their way to make sure that you get to spend time with your kids and make partner.

As of the summer of 2011, Kristen thought partnership might be an option at some point, but the firm did not have a stated partnership track.

As a small firm, there was no precedence for her to see a light at the end of the tunnel. She commented, "I am not really holding my breath." She was also concerned that partnership would increase the firm's expectations of her without making a financial difference. Although Kristen was not overtly positive about making partner, she also felt that it would happen at some point in the future. She stated, "I assume that at some point it will happen. It will be great. I don't see any point in pressing it." She also did not intend to leave her firm, as they are very supportive of her needs in regard to her family and notes, "I think that is rare."

Only six months later, Kristen gave the following update regarding partnership and pregnancy,

> I was promoted to partner in December, which was particularly surprising given that I am six months pregnant. I guess it sort of goes against what I would have expected. When the partners told me, I mentioned that I appreciated the timing given the pregnancy, and my boss said (with a sarcastic undertone), "Oh yeah—I had forgotten you were pregnant." So regardless of the motivation behind it (which still baffles me a bit), I think it still says something positive about opportunities for women at smaller firms and in intellectual property in particular.

Kristen was happy to take this next step in her career, particularly at a time when her pregnancy might have been seen as a liability. She was very open with the firm about her desire to have a third child. Once pregnant, Kristen has morning sickness, so it is difficult for her to conceal a pregnancy for any length of time. She realized that having another child could hinder her career; however, she was undaunted:

> In the back of my mind, having another kid is more important to me than anything that has to do with my career. Really. So if someone wants to punish me for that, or they were going to make me partner and aren't now because I am going to have a third kid, that really doesn't matter.

Happily, Kristen was not punished for having a third child; on the contrary, her work and commitment to the firm spoke for itself. This recognition is important to her, as she states, "Being a partner is something that shows that you are doing a good job."

| Advice: Business development is critical to success |

As a law firm partner now, Kristen must pay close attention to business development. By obtaining her own clients, she will have more autonomy over her schedule. This might allow her to work from home and see the kids after school as the years progress. Kristen also regards her bachelor's degree in Biology as challenging for business development in her field. Some inventors/clients prefer specialized, advanced degrees in the scientific area at issue for a patent application. Kristen has had success working with individual inventors but notes the cost of taking on such clients. She has to take time educating them and helping to develop the invention to the point of submitting it in a patent application. Individual clients cannot always completely compensate her for her time because they are generally start-ups. She comments, "There is a lot of pressure at work to be bringing in larger corporate clients."

Kristen has had success getting referrals from her work on the state and local bar associations. In addition, her clients are glad to give out her name. Kristen notes, "I work really well with my clients. I have great relationships with my clients." She feels that word of mouth will eventually go to the right kind of corporate client and then she will have the opportunity to demonstrate her skills. However, her big struggle right now is business development with the type of client that the firm wants.

Kristen has had to make sacrifices in terms of spending the extra time developing business. Because of her family obligations, she can't always be out three or four nights a week working on meeting potential clients. She comments, "There is more stuff that I could be doing that I can't do anymore." She continues to serve on bar association boards, and so forth, but she worries that she could be out trying to meet more people.

She also has made sacrifices in spending time with her family. With her sons now five and three and with a new baby on the way, she can reflect on her time as a working mom:

> It has gone by so quickly. I look back at their baby books, and I did such a poor job doing all that and putting all of that together. . . . Sometimes I feel like I have missed parts of them growing up already, and it goes by way too quickly. I worry that they are going to be eighteen, and I am going to look back and think, "Where did it go?" I don't know if that is any different whether you work or not work, because I am sure it goes quickly for everybody, but I feel like I have sacrificed part of experiencing them as children just based on the scheduling and trying to fit everything in.

> Advice: Take time out for yourself.

One area that Kristen has not sacrificed is her own health and mental wellness. After she had her first son, Kristen began running, eventually losing fifty pounds and finding a form of mental release that keeps her sane.

> I will be very tied up about something, stressed about something, worried about something, overwhelmed about something, and then I will go run and I come back and it is like "everything is okay." It takes the edge off, and the endorphins it produces help to counteract the stress. It clears my head. It tires you out physically, so you can think more clearly. I don't know the mechanism by which it does it. As I run, I can sometimes work through things in my head. It has become cathartic and something I can't live without.

Every day, Kristen takes at least thirty minutes to run. She has a running group at her office that reinforces her commitment. This allows her to carve out the time without any excuses for something that makes her feel terrific.

Kristen also makes time for a local mentorship program with law school students. She gives her mentee the advice not to necessarily delay having a family to focus on a career. In her opinion, many women feel that they need to wait until they have worked for a few years before they can dare have children. Kristen notes that there are other options:

> I didn't plan it this way and I would have never planned it this way, but I started out part time and it was ideal. I was part time when I was pregnant with my first, having my first, and for most of his first year. . . . While financially it was a struggle, it actually worked out great. There are lots of different ways you can do it, and it does not have to be set in stone that you have to work for a couple years, then decide to have kids.

From Kristen's perspective, having the right support at home and at work are the most important factors in making it all work. From that base of support, a woman can feel like a success at work and at home. In her opinion, firms need to recognize that women can be serious lawyers and successful, caring parents, and the two roles are not mutually exclusive.

> One of the things that drives me in the legal field is the opportunity to progress. . . . I don't think that many firms give you that opportunity. I think that once you go to have kids, you are looked at differently. You don't have the opportunity, and your likelihood of becoming a partner is that much less. Generally, the mentality is, "You have to make a choice."

Kristen's ascension to partner at her firm and role as a mother to her children demonstrates that it can be done. For Kristen, a smaller firm has been the right fit.

Chapter Five

REALISTIC EXPECTATIONS AND THE SMALL-FIRM MOM

"Find a husband that can cook and clean and likes to do it too. It is a tough struggle that a lot of those responsibilities still fall on women's shoulders even if they are successful working mom attorneys."
—Kristie Cary Fingerhut

KRISTIE CARY FINGERHUT ATTENDED the University of Southern California majoring in Psychology and minoring in Law and Society, knowing that her end goal was law school. She went on to Loyola University School of Law graduating in 2003. After graduation, Kristie landed a coveted clerkship with the Cook County Circuit Court in Chicago, working on the commercial docket. As she contemplated her next move, she knew that children were in her future, but not immediately.

In 2004 she applied to a small family law firm north of Chicago run by a father and son partner team. There were three men but no women working at the firm. Kristie knew she had to get information at her first interview about how the firm might handle it if she decided to start a family. She broached the subject saying, "I know you are looking for someone long term. There are no women working at the firm. This is not an immediate issue, but what is your maternity leave policy?" The two men generally responded that they would take it one step at a time, replying, "Well, we will have to see how valuable you are when that becomes an issue, and we will address it at that time."

Though this might not have been the response Kristie wanted, she felt the firm was a good fit and that she would be able to get valuable hands-on experience working at a small firm. She was also well aware that the firm did not have to comply with the Family Medical Leave Act in granting her a maternity leave because of its small size. Two years later, she found out she was expecting. She told the firm at nine weeks so that they could begin to craft a maternity policy. She had become instrumental in the firm. The father was travelling more, and Kristie was taking over more work. The firm wanted to keep her but was juggling how to deal with the maternity leave issue.

Kristie also had to reassure them that she was going to return to the firm after her maternity leave. After asking them "a million times" about the maternity policy, and demonstrating that she was able to work through her pregnancy, they told her that they were going to pay for a portion of her maternity leave, but they weren't sure how much yet.

With this in mind, Kristie had her daughter in November of 2006. The firm allowed her to take seven weeks off paid, as she would have returned at six weeks during the week of Christmas. She notes, "As a first-time mother, I would have loved to have had twelve weeks off." However, she felt lucky that they paid her salary for seven weeks.

Additionally, they allowed her time to transition back to the office. She returned on a full-time basis after the New Year, but the firm allowed her to work in the office three days a week and at home two days a week. Kristie worked partially from home until her daughter was four and a half months old. She initiated her full return to the office, commenting,

> I am the one that initiated the return to full time, five days in the office, more because it was most stressful for me to be home and try to work those two days and get enough work done to stay productive

and helpful to them. I understand as an associate that was my primary role to make their job easier, and if I wasn't making their job easier, then I wasn't performing my job.

Kristie wanted to make the decision to return to the office on a five-day basis before they asked her to make the switch. She also found that she could compartmentalize her life more easily by having her daughter in full-time day care.

Ironically, Kristie notes that the two years after her having her first daughter were some of her best. She relates, "Looking back now, that year and the next year were two of my most productive years to date." She credits the economy to a point, and that having a child forced her to be efficient with her time. However, she is now reflecting on those years and asking herself why those years were so productive, something she is focused on continuing.

Kristie's second daughter was born in April of 2009. She took six weeks off, then returned to the firm full time. Having two small children has been a challenge, especially when things don't go according to plan. One of her biggest challenges is when the children are ill and cannot go to daycare. She queries, "What do you do when your kid wakes up with a fever, and you have to be in court?" On days that she can, she will work from home. She and her husband might even tag team, with Kristie working from home in the morning, and he in the afternoon, when possible. They also learned that her husband's company had a hidden benefit—the company will subsidize on-call daycare. His company actually pays 66 percent of on-call expenses for a caregiver to come to their home up to 100 hours. Kristie is not comfortable using the on-call daycare all the time—essentially it is still a stranger coming to her home. However, they have taken advantage of this benefit in a pinch. Kristie also has had success in developing a network of stay-at-home moms who can act as a backup when she needs it.

Kristie has also struggled with trying to meet the needs of her demanding practice area. Litigation, particularly family law litigation, is a high-passion, high-conflict area of law. Though she tries to mediate and settle cases, she still has to prepare for trial and be ready to litigate frequently. With this type of caseload, it can be difficult to resolve her work day by 5:00 p.m. to make it to daycare for pickup. She comments that women who pursue litigation may have to adjust their own expectations about juggling career and family:

If you want to be that stay-at-home mom that is there when the bus drops off at 2:00 p.m. every day, it is probably not going to be a good fit for you unless you can find a job share or a part-time place where you can largely work from home. Most careers that involve litigation, which has largely been my experience, are very time-demanding, and you can't necessarily fit it all in between 8:00 a.m. and 2:00 p.m. when the kids are in school. Depositions have to be taken, court dates are in the afternoon, trials are in the afternoon. You just can't do that. If your expectations are adjusted to accommodate for that, I think that it can be a good thing, but it is demanding.

Whether we want to or not, stereotypically in my experience and my friends that I have observed, moms are still expected to do the lion share of the traditional mom tasks whether or not they are working as attorneys during the day. That is hard to squeeze everything in because there are only so many hours in the day. You have to be willing to give up in some of those areas in order to make it all work.

Advice: Use technology to your advantage.

Kristie credits technology with helping her manage her workload. Even ten years ago, she could not be the attorney she is today because of the advances in technology. She logs into her computer at home once the kids go to sleep. Many of her clients receive documents at odd hours—sometimes 1:00 a.m. Kristie is lucky to be able to function well on little sleep.

Despite the challenges of being a working mom, Kristie likes the advantage of working at a small firm. She feels like she has more flexibility than some of her large-firm counterparts. Additionally, she doesn't have to deal with the same type of hierarchy and demands on her time in terms of business development and "face time." In the early stages of her career, Kristie knew that ultimately her priority was not climbing a career ladder but raising a family while having a satisfying career:

We were going to have a family, and that was part of the plan. I didn't go to law school so I could go on partnership track at a big law firm. That helped identify really more my goals and set my plan at that point. I would say that the largest advantage is being able to have more flexibility.

Kristie also appreciates that the partners in her firm are parents themselves, though they may not have the same concerns she does as a working mom with very small children:

> I was fortunate at my firm that the partners themselves have kids or had kids at home at some point. So they understand to some degree the rigors and demands of [parenthood], so that made it a little easier to transition.

Kristie also has reasonable billable hour requirements. The firm asks her to bill 1,500 hours on an annual basis. She has been able to meet those goals, with the exception of the years when she had her children and during a particularly rough year when her kids were sick on a regular basis. The firm understood, and Kristie tried to work from home as much as she could to keep things running: however, her bonus reflected her decrease in hours. This year Kristie is back on target and happy that the firm saw her through those times:

> It makes me really appreciate my job a lot more knowing that some of my counterparts from law school at big firms in the city are working 2,000–2,100 hours or whatever. I would not be able to go to my kids' preschool events.

As the small firm has advantages, it also has some disadvantages. As the only associate, work can pile up when Kristie has been out of the office. During her first maternity leave, the accumulation of work made for a very stressful few weeks upon her return. When she had her second daughter, the firm chose to bring in another associate to keep up on discovery and other matters. The firm was busier at that point, and her role had expanded to the point where she was missed more. Working in such a small firm, Kristie has less backup at the office than she would have in a larger office. She also notes that as the only female attorney in the office with small children, her situation is unique:

> It is difficult in some aspects because again the men in my office have wives at home to do a lot of the tasks that I do at home too. I joke that I need a wife a lot of the time because it would make my life a lot easier.

Advice: Pull in extra help when you need it.

She has had to adjust her family life to deal with the pressures of her demanding job, but Kristie has also realized that she does not have to be the only person who does everything for her kids. One strategy she has employed is hiring extra help two nights a week. Essentially, on Tuesdays and Thursdays, a babysitter picks up her girls from daycare and provides the services of a night nanny. She feeds them dinner, gets them bathed and in their pajamas, and puts them to sleep. Having two nights during the week to catch up on work, and the occasional trip to the grocery store, allows Kristie's life to run more smoothly and has reduced her personal stress level immensely. Although Kristie feels validated that with this extra help she can get more done and not fall behind, she still struggles with her own feelings about the situation:

> I do feel guilt sometimes about that because I am having someone put the kids to bed two nights a week. Why should it be any different for me when my husband has me put the kids to bed five nights a week? Why should I feel guilty for hiring someone so I can work like he does?

Given the flexible work arrangement that she has found, Kristie feels that she is able to give her kids the best of both worlds, particularly since she doesn't think she is cut out to be a stay-at-home mom, noting:

> I like my kids. I love my kids. I like my time that I get to spend with them on vacations and such, but I am a much better mom when I am working.

She further comments, "Every mom is going to feel guilty about something." In her opinion, stay-at-home moms feel guilty about leaving their kids too. As she has seen her children grow and develop, she is encouraged by the fact that they are very social and outgoing and attributes it to the fact that they have had exposure to other people.

Kristie also feels that her kids have largely benefited from being in their particular daycare and that it has been helpful in getting a routine established. She is able to compartmentalize her work and home life in this manner:

> I try to work hard when I am at work and not work so much when I am at home, at least when they are awake. I think that I am able to enjoy the best parts and appreciate the parts when I am at home and

with them rather than just getting frazzled by it. I think we are all benefiting from that, and they are getting to enjoy many other experiences and other things that are able come from the fact that both parents are working and have the income to do other activities, such as travelling. . . .

Being the only female attorney at the firm, Kristie has had to blaze her own trail as a working mom. She has been fortunate to have a group of legal moms that she has met through the bar association who share the same concerns in juggling family with their careers. They are able to complain and commiserate, and essentially act as mentors for each other. It has been inspiring to her that the women of this group continued practicing after having children. They have also been able to help each other in setting expectations among firms about workplace policies:

> We are all still practicing. I think it is in part because there are so many of us that are doing it. Some of the other "bosses" have sort of made accommodations that maybe they wouldn't have otherwise made, but because they knew that one of the other bosses had done that. All of us have pretty much had six weeks of paid maternity leave because it has sort of become the norm around here.

Despite the difficulties associated with juggling a career and family, Kristie believes that law can be a good career for a mom, as long as a woman can adjust her expectations. She also agrees that the statistic that 25 percent of female attorneys leave the legal profession after having their first child is pretty accurate, noting that it is not a profession that is necessarily conducive to flexibility:

> In large part, it is the demands placed on moms who are working moms in the legal environment. Even if employers want to give you flexibility and want to help provide accommodations to allow you to have kids, there is still only so much you can do. When you've got to get a case out the door and a trial to prepare for, there is just only so much that can be done within the practice of law to accommodate for that. . . . This places a lot of demands on moms.

She further notes that litigation places additional expectations on attorneys, regardless of gender or parenting status:

When the courthouse is open and conducting business between 9:00 a.m. and 5:00 p.m., as an attorney working there, you are expected to be able to show up for trial when they schedule them as opposed to when you might need them scheduled. That is something that nobody can accommodate for unless you are going to be an attorney who does not try cases.

Kristie has certainly made sacrifices in her attempts to blend a career and family life. Foremost in her mind has been sleep. During the week and weekends, she is primarily the parent who wakes up with the kids. She tries to make time for personal hobbies, such as scrapbooking and card making, but the time is limited that she has to herself. Because her career is such a large part of her life, it was always important for her to find the right fit, and she was conscious of her own priorities from the beginning of her career:

> You hear a lot about attorneys of any gender of any practice area burning out after so many years and just not liking their jobs. I didn't go to law school and incur all the hard work and loans that I did to get out of [the practice of law] after five years. I was looking for something that was going to be sustainable. I was very fortunate just to fall into this position where they were looking for someone who was going to be around for a while who was going to be a long-term part of the office. That was helpful.
>
> Because I didn't have kids at the time, I was conscious of the fact that if something needed to get done I didn't have to rush home . . . so I was willing to put in the hours. I would tell them, "I don't have daycare right now to rush to; if you need this done, I will sit here and do it." I think that earned some points too within the office to allow me that flexibility later when I did need it. They know that I am willing to get the work done. It may get done at 1:00 in the morning, but it will get done. They can trust me with that. I think that was somewhat helpful.

As Kristie takes a step back and thinks about her own career and family life, she reflects that as a society we need to adjust our marketing strategy about career life to young women. Not that we should discourage them from pursuing their dreams, but that we need to give them a more realistic picture of how much work it requires. Borrowing from others, she generally comments that you can do it all, but it is not always possible to do everything all at the same time. One issue that she particularly notices is that working moms are still expected to do what stay-at-home moms do while also maintaining a career. In her opinion, this has elicited a lot more stress than what she expected. Kristie wishes she had been given more advice in this regard before she chose to take out substantial student loans and pursue law school—not that she would have made different choices, but she would have been more aware.

> Advice: Look into a legal career (thoroughly) before you leap.

Kristie would advise women to do their homework before pursuing a legal career. Knowing the expectations of the particular practice area that you are pursuing can make a big difference with work-life balance issues later:

> You have to set realistic expectations and goals. Do your research in finding an area of law that would be more conducive to your wants and desires and what you want to do with your family life. Some areas like litigation aren't going to be as flexible.

At this point, Kristie is happy with her own career trajectory. As time passes, she would like to take on more of her own clients and perhaps become partner with her current firm. She is okay with the idea of being an employee now while her kids are young, but as they become more independent, she sees herself pursuing more work independently. She is proud of the career and life she has built and believes it has impacted her own children positively:

> Especially since I have two daughters, it is helpful to show them a strong role model. I don't know that I will advise them to go to law school or recommend that to them someday. It is a lot of work, and I don't think that I realized how much work it would be to be a working mom when I set out on this path. I wouldn't give it up, but I don't know if I would necessarily do it all over again.

Kristie's own blend of realism and hard work has paid off, as both her career and family life are working for her. She is happy at work and proud of her family life. On a final note, she cautions against the ideal standard of perfection, commenting, "You are never going to be able to do everything all the time as perfectly as you may want to because there are only so many hours in the day." Sound advice for moms everywhere.

Part Two

THE CORPORATE WORLD

Chapter Six

A LEGAL CAREER
ON THE RISE

*"The only real accomplishment that I could have in this world would
be to raise good kids who contribute to the world."*
—*Anne-Marie Kennedy*

CHOOSING THE RIGHT LUNCH can change your life. Anne-Marie Kennedy is proof that sandwiches can be linked to destiny. Working as a corporate and commercial real estate associate at a mid-sized Chicago law firm, she was the only female associate in her project group. Immediately out of Notre Dame College of Law, she made a very conscious decision to join this particular firm because she believed they were committed to work-life balance and were family friendly. Anne-Marie knew that she eventually wanted a family and was cognizant that the decisions she made would matter eventually.

When looking at law firms, she heeded advice given to her by a friend's father who was a lawyer. He told her, if given the option, going to the largest law firm may not be the best choice. He specifically counseled her to look at the quality of the work and whether she would be able to have some sort of life. Anne-Marie recalls visiting the firm and noting that many of the attorneys had artwork from their kids hanging in their offices. She felt that this firm was not all about billable hours. She now describes her initial impression as naïve.

> On the surface I was aware of those issues, I think I was naïve though. I felt like all I needed to do to be successful was really good work and be a good person. And even though I knew about these billable hours and they told me what their billable hour requirement was, I didn't think to ask, "So what are your average billable hours?"—that next question. I didn't think to myself that this is a business and the widget that I was going to be producing would be my billable hour. That was an "aha moment" once I got to the firm.

In her third year at the firm, she knew she was generally unhappy. She was working all the time and did not have the personal life she wanted. She was doing well at the firm professionally, but began to think, "Yes, I can do it if I put my mind to it, but do I want to?" Anne-Marie was also worried that if she continued the way she was headed, she would never have the personal life she wanted, especially as she saw friends and coworkers get married and have children.

Eventually, she came to the realization that she didn't really like what she was doing and that part of her unhappiness was that the people with whom she worked were not happy either. As she looked around, there was nobody at the firm who had carved a path that Anne-Marie saw for herself.

> I couldn't identify with any of the female partners at the firm. They fell into one of two boats. They either were extremely successful, and I admired what they had accomplished professionally . . . but they had disastrous personal lives. They were divorced or had one child who was raised full time by nannies and really no relationship with that child. Or alternatively, there were women that I really genuinely liked more, but I felt like they weren't really "important." At that point, I think "important" was important to me. . . . They had a normal family life, but I felt like they were always on the verge of being let go, not because they weren't good lawyers. . . . There were not any shareholder female partners that had personal lives that I wanted for myself.

Here is where lunch changed Anne-Marie's life. She decided to grab a sandwich at the local sandwich place, Potbellies. While in line, she saw a chalkboard sign that read,

Hey! If you are an attorney with 3–5 years of Commercial Real Estate or General Corporate Experience, go to monsterjobs.com and look us up.

She went back to her office and went to www.monsterjobs.com. The first posting she saw said, "Fortune 500 company seeks commercial real estate attorney with 3–5 years experience in the Chicagoland area. If interested, please submit your resume." She ultimately submitted her resume and learned that the job was with a larger restaurant chain.

> Advice: Sometimes opportunities arise when you aren't looking. Keep your eyes open.

In discussing the job with the headhunter and her concerns about going forward in the interview process, the headhunter asked her, "Are you really happy with what you are doing?" Anne-Marie started to cry. She knew that she had to make a change. Two weeks later, she had the job. Some of the partners at the firm told her that she was making a critical mistake. Her response was, "If it is a mistake, so what?—I am only 27 years old."

Despite what her firm cautioned, moving to a corporate position was a great move for Anne-Marie. Her career took off. She gives some of the credit to the fact that for the first time she had female mentors who understood her and provided examples of how to succeed in law and in life. Anne-Marie's career turned around when she found female mentors who understood her.

> I don't think women do other women any favors by sugar-coating how hard this is. Generally speaking, women are not supportive of other women. We need to be more supportive of each other.

The culture was very different at an in-house environment. She was getting "thank yous" for just doing her job, and she really liked it. She was also fortunate to start her job the same day that another prominent female attorney started, who would ultimately become a mentor. This woman had been an equity partner at a large firm and had come from another corporate in-house counsel position. She had two daughters and a full-time nanny. Anne-Marie describes her as a unique woman because she truly felt that she had done it the hard way but that it didn't need to be that way for the next generation of female lawyers. She sought out Anne-Marie multiple times for lunch, and they hit it off. She became a trusted mentor to Anne-Marie, which became crucial when she dealt with some initial issues in corporate restructuring. This mentor ultimately put her in a position to work with outstanding people where she continued to develop and work on exciting projects.

> Advice: Not all in-house positions are created equal. In a corporate position, it matters very much more with whom you work.

In the mix of advancing her corporate career, Anne-Marie found time to fall in love and get married in 2007. In October of 2009, she welcomed a son, taking off four months of maternity leave.

She returned to the office in February and describes the transition as hard. Her first business trip was scheduled for March with her direct boss, the General Counsel for the Eastern Region. He had been very supportive during her maternity leave and was impressed with her work product and work ethic. It was fortunate that he was a father of three, especially during a particularly uncomfortable situation at the airport.

Anne-Marie took this first trip about a month after returning to work. She was still nursing her son, so she travelled with her breast pump. During her departure trip, there were no issues. However, on the return, she was travelling with several containers of breast milk. With her boss behind her in the security line, the agent at the airport became concerned because the liquid she was carrying weighed more than the ounces allowed by Homeland Security. She tried to explain quietly that it was breast milk, which he did not seem to comprehend. As she averted any eye contact with her boss, the agent individually scanned each packet of breast milk and Anne-Marie tried to conceal feeling absolutely horrified. Neither she nor her boss acknowledged that this happened, which was a great relief to her. In considering all of the issues she would have returning to work, this situation had not crossed her mind.

It was during this trip that her boss told her he was moving to Singapore to take over the Asia-Pacific Region for the company. Anne-Marie was not happy about the change because he had been instrumental to her development. Having just returned from leave, she was also concerned about working for someone else. However, he indicated that she was under serious consideration for his job. She would be the youngest person rising to the position of General Counsel of the Eastern Division of the corporation, answering to the General Counsel for North America—essentially one step from the top.

Although excited about the opportunity, she was unsure whether or not to pursue it. Having just had her son, she felt that the timing could not have been worse. Anne-Marie was hesitant because she wasn't yet operating at full speed. Her son was a difficult baby, she wasn't sleeping through the night, and sometimes she couldn't finish her sentences. Her mind raced to whether she could take on additional career responsibilities being so new to motherhood.

She took some time to think about it. The job required additional travel and management of a staff of fourteen people. Ultimately, she decided to go for it. She competed against twenty people for the position. When she got the job, her first concern was that the company had based their decision on her pre-baby performance, and she was worried she would disappoint them. Her second concern was related to self-doubt. She asked herself "Can I really do this?"

Self-doubt might be a common character trait of Type-A personalities; however, Anne-Marie was not only concerned about how she could manage this new job but how she could juggle her responsibilities as a mother with this demanding new job. She struggles with feeling that she is not operating at 100 percent at work or at home.

She travels on average every two weeks, trying to limit her time away to one or two nights. It bothers her that her son is usually still asleep when she leaves the house at 7:00 a.m. But at this point, she does not feel like she has control over her schedule because her role requires her to be involved in so many aspects of the company. She generally tries to leave the office by 6:00 p.m., but depending on the situation at work, she can sometimes be working until 8:00 or 9:00. If her schedule continues this way, she worries that it will not be sustainable, especially if she chooses to have another child.

Anne-Marie is at a crossroads of her career at thirty-four years old. Her intelligence and quality of work have ensured her ascension up the corporate ladder, but she is beginning to question whether the sacrifices she is making personally are worth it to her. She has considered going part time, but struggles with what this will mean to her career. She worries that she has "capped out" at her position, because she may not be able to sustain the sacrifices she needs to make. However, if she were to go part time, would she be out of contention forever for additional positions? It comes back to where her priorities ultimately lie.

> I'm always so afraid that I will be counted out if I am not just as good as, if not better than, my male counterparts or these other women who seem to be able to do it all.

Part of Anne-Marie's struggle is her belief that the optimal environment for her son would be for her to stay home with him full time, or even part time. Financially, she has the ability to stay home and sometimes feels guilty about needing her career to validate her. She likes and needs the external gratification that work provides. Anne-Marie does not think it is necessarily healthy for families to have two parents pursuing full-time demanding careers. She admires women who stay home with their children because it is really hard. However, she acknowledges that she probably idealizes what it might be like to stay home. She likes the monetary benefits and socialization that her career provides.

She credits her son with helping her to switch gears from work. She has become better at separating work and home, instead of ruminating about issues at work. She misses her son while she is working, but she implicitly trusts the people watching him during the day—her mom and a part-time nanny.

Last fall, she had three weeks of almost constant travel, and she ultimately cut her last trip short because she missed her son so tremendously. It was at this point that she called on the stable of female mentors she has cultivated. Each of them understood her feelings and encouraged her to create boundaries. In her position, it is easy to fall into the trap of thinking that every meeting is crucial. Anne-Marie is in a process of discerning her own boundaries—a difficult task for a self-described Type A person.

Advice: Create boundaries and don't provide excuses for having a reasonable personal life.

Clearly, a key to Anne-Marie's success has been the fact that she has sought out women whom she admired personally and professionally. She credits them with some of the best advice she has received and that she now gives to other women. Particularly, there is no right or wrong way to raise children. She has also learned to try to let go of things and not stress out as much. Her mentors have recognized that they cannot always be 100 percent but that you do the best you can. She recalls an incident when her son hit his head and now has a scar. Anne-Marie tortures herself that if she had gotten home sooner, it would not have happened, but ultimately knows that she cannot control every situation.

> Advice: Seek out women whom you admire for guidance and encouragement.

Anne-Marie also credits Maria Shriver as an influence as she struggles with work-life balance issues. Anne-Marie graduated from the College of the Holy Cross in 1998 where Maria Shriver delivered the famous commencement address that developed into the book *Ten Things I Wish I Knew before I Went out into the Real World*. Although some of the sentiments were lost on 21-year old Anne-Marie, she looks back on the speech and realizes how "dead-on" the advice was, particularly the phrase "Superwoman is Dead." Appearances are not all they are chalked up to be, and something has to give. Raising children while having a demanding career is simply not easy.

However, it has always been important to Anne-Marie to be "important" in some way. She wants to be considered as a contender. At the same time, she is starting to realize that the external stuff in her life might be superficial and that her family is her most important part of her life. The only thing that holds her back from going part time is herself, but she worries about how others would perceive it. She acknowledges that her own self-worth is based on external motivators. She is now feeling that her career might not be the best thing for her family, but she worries that she could lose great work that she likes doing. She does feel very fortunate that her company does not treat women like second-class citizens, and there are many examples of women who happily work part time.

Ultimately, Anne-Marie's most important female mentor was her own mother, a stay-at-home mom who had aspirations for more. Her mother was a nurse who put herself through college and was interested in pursuing an MBA. She was accepted at the Kellogg School of Business at Northwestern University but decided not to pursue the degree because she was in the midst of raising children. She promoted and pushed Anne-Marie to have a fulfilling career. Anne-Marie quotes the phrase, "You can do anything, but you can't do it all at the same time." She wants to have a fulfilling legal career but also wants to spend more time with her son and be a great mother. Juggling these roles competing for her time has been hard.

Anne-Marie has thought about how society can keep more women at the table who want to pursue a legal career and raise children:

> The obvious answer is to provide more flexible work arrangements, but we have flexible work arrangements at my company. The people who are considered "up and comers" do not take advantage of flexible hours. There would have to be a precedent set. There would have to be women in leadership roles who continue to rise in the ranks while they are participating in flexible work arrangements and setting boundaries for themselves.

Essentially, companies and firms would have to stop rewarding the behavior of working all weekend. Anne-Marie currently supervises a mom who works four days a week. When Anne-Marie asked her why she didn't pursue more advanced positions within the company, she responded that she would like to advance at some point, but while her children are young, they are her priority. Anne-Marie has made it clear that as her supervisor she is trying to set an example of rewarding someone for excellent work, despite personal circumstances that allow for a flexible work arrangement.

Anne-Marie believes the law is a good career for a mother—the struggles of female attorneys raising children are not exclusive to the legal profession. Women in other professions face the same difficult choices. Although she feels that law firms are not particularly conducive to having a fulfilling personal life, specifically because of the billable hour structure.

She is unsure about her career goals at this point. She wants to continue doing meaningful work and be recognized for it. She wants to be valued but is unsure how important it is for her to continue ascending the corporate ranks. She hopes to have a happy, healthy family. At times it seems to her that as her career goals have waned, her life goals have become more developed.

> When I am gone, nobody is going to care what I ever did at [the corporation] what kept me at the office until 8:30 or 9:00 at night, or where I travelled, or who I met, or how much money I had. The only real legacy I will have is my child.

Anne-Marie gives the following advice to women who want to raise children while pursuing a legal career:

- Make sure that you are conscious of the choices you are making. As long as you are conscious about the choices you are making, you can be satisfied with them. Evaluate the sacrifices you are making.
- You have to set your own boundaries and parameters, rather than allowing someone else to do so. Your boss may require certain performance or expect you to work a particular number of hours. If you choose to do so, recognize what you might be giving up on the personal side. If you choose not to do so, know that it may hurt you professionally. Be conscious of your decisions.
- At the end of the day, it is your life and your career. Whatever decisions or choices you make will be the right ones for you and your family.
- As women, we have an obligation to bring other women along. As you advance, mentor other women and promote their work.

Chapter Seven

FROM LAW
FIRM MOM TO
IN-HOUSE MOM

*"We should continue to believe that we have the ability
to do both. The only way that we will be able to do that
successfully over time is if more of us stick it out. . . .
We have to stay in the game."*

—Ama Romaine

AMA ROMAINE WANTED TO BE A LAWYER for as long as she can remember. As a child, she was often frustrated by injustice. Because of her strong moral compass, she wanted to study law to right the wrongs in the world. This desire could have translated into a career as a prosecutor or a civil rights attorney. However, another facet of her personality—her hatred of public speaking—took her down another career path in the law.

As a Canadian of Caribbean descent, Ama attended York University in Toronto, then headed to Howard University School of Law in Washington, DC, where she was awarded a full scholarship.

Her first position upon graduation was in the DC office of a large New York-based law firm. Children were the furthest thing from her mind. Her focus was on practicing international law. Having lived in Trinidad and Toronto, Ama was keen on working for a firm that dealt with exciting international issues. She started her position in September and in a turn of events was pregnant with her first child by May.

She had a positive experience as a working mom at her firm and credits her boss, who was married to a partner at another firm with a part-time schedule, and female mentors who were instrumental in helping her manage her career. She saw several women successfully juggling career and family, which emboldened her as she embarked on motherhood.

> As I move through my career, I am always looking for that place where I feel like I can be a professional and also be a mother. I want both, and I don't feel like they have to be mutually exclusive. . . . I think a lot of it has to do with that very first experience, where I saw women who were really successful and were balancing. . . . I think that gave me a sense of entitlement that it can work.

On the advice of one of her mentors, Ama chose to wait five years to have another child. Anecdotally, Ama felt that young women of color tended to have their children earlier in life, which could be harder on their careers, especially a legal career. In regard to how law firms deal with motherhood, Ama remarks,

> The environment does not embrace mothers in the workplace. They will embrace women in the workplace, who happen to be mothers, but not really mothers. If you have young children, and you are also relatively young in your career, it is hard to separate those out.

Advice: At work, present a professional front.

As she progresses in her career, Ama has become more aware of separating her roles as a mother and a lawyer. There was a time when she did not have pictures of her children at the office. She tempers how much she talks about her children. She prefers not to connect her reasons for leaving the office to her children. In her opinion, women are able to be more successful in the workplace if their colleagues see them as women and professionals first, rather than mothers.

Ama's perspective developed from her own personal experience. As a law student, she recalls talking with a fellow classmate who was pregnant during interview season. Ama's friend was concerned about keeping her impending motherhood quiet, noting that this was something that really could hurt her chances at a job. Ama was incredulous and asked her, "Why would you want to work anywhere that wouldn't want you if you are a mother anyway?" She reflects on this statement as naïve.

Ama left her first firm to work internationally in Trinidad for a year. When she returned to the United States, she sought out non-law firm jobs, but found an interesting pattern in her interviews. When asked why she was not returning to a law firm, in the interviews where she mentioned her daughter, she was not given a job offer. For those interviews where she did not mention that she had a child, she received job offers. She felt that all of the interviews went very well, and certainly correlation is not causation, but nevertheless she noticed this trend. In retrospect, she now agrees with her law school friend—it does not pay for women to speak about children in an interview or excessively in the workplace.

Ama eventually made the decision to return to big law in Washington, DC, but on a full-time basis. At her first law firm, she had worked a 60 percent schedule, but felt that it was part-time pay for full-time work. It seemed that the work came in only on the days that she was not scheduled to be in the office, so she was consistently putting in hours at home to make it work. She was disappointed at this idiosyncrasy and decided that she would work full time. She found out she was pregnant with her second child the day she accepted the offer from the firm where she was to work.

At this new large firm, with a second child, her career took over. In her words, "My son didn't even know me. I was his least favorite person in the family. I was out twelve to fourteen hours a day." Ama's mother lives with her family, which allowed Ama the ability to focus on her career. "I really just have an incredible support base. There is no way I could do what I am doing at work successfully without having that kind of support at home."

She ultimately decided to leave the firm because she found that her family life was suffering, which in turn caused her work life to suffer.

The impetus to leave my second firm was the result of not feeling like I was excelling at home or at work and this was untenable.

She had relinquished some of the nighttime duties to her husband because she was so exhausted from working a full-time schedule and felt that her son had bonded with her daughter, her husband, and her mother, but not with her. She felt as if she was the person he saw at the end of the day for a short time but wasn't always so interested in seeing her. She reflects,

> There is a question that I sometimes ask myself; if this were my last day on earth, would I want to know that this was how I spent my last day? The answer to that question was always NO.

It was difficult for Ama to put the brakes on her career. As a young woman, she was looking toward the future of her career—partnership and advancement. However, she realized that the race she was running need not be a sprint:

> A lot of the women that I really respected and admired had been practicing for a really long time. They didn't get there five years or ten years out of school. I realized that I had time on that front that I didn't necessarily have the time in the same way with my kids because I would just never get back some of this time that I was losing. Once it's gone, it's gone. I need to start looking for something that will allow me to feel better about myself and the decisions that I am making.

Ama started looking for in-house jobs believing that the hours might still be long, but there could be greater opportunity for balance. The timing was very good. Within a few weeks, she had a job offer. She chose to work for a major hotel corporation, which was conveniently located ten minutes from her home and her daughter's school. This met her need to be more present to her kids.

Advice: Consider how a commute will affect your quality of life.

Ama realized quickly how much time she had lost commuting over the years and how much a long commute impacted the quality of her life. In the time she saved commuting, she was not only able to spend more time with her children but also was able to give herself some "me" time including exercising regularly, gardening and generally taking better care of herself. She was able to step out and visit her daughter's school during her lunch hour without stressing out. She could make it to after-work events by 5:30, leaving the office at 5:20.

Despite her dream commute, Ama was presented with an opportunity with a similar yet larger corporation and chose to take it. Although she left the law firm to create more balance in her life, she was unwilling to "flatline" her career. She wanted an upward trajectory and the chance to advance and develop. This was a difficult decision because it meant that she would be back to a more difficult commute.

Reflecting on this moment in her carreer, Ama recalls a graduation address at Barnard College by Cheryl Sandberg, the chief operating officer of Facebook for inspiring her to "lean into her career." She notes that more often than not, women opt out of great opportunities because they fear that they will not be able to balance their roles. Ama has followed Sandberg's advice not to count herself out, but rather to work hard and assess each situation as it presents itself.

Her new position has been challenging (and requires a longer commute); however, she has gotten everything she wanted professionally out of this career move, which has been great for her personally. Part of her comfort level with the transition is that she has more experience at this point to reflect upon:

> I am a little older and I can trust myself. I feel like I know I work really hard. I will do whatever it takes to get the best job done that I can. Even if it means working, leaving, going home, dealing with my kids, putting them to bed, and signing back on and working some more. I do that quite a bit. That does get draining. It makes me feel good because I know that I am putting in an honest day's work for an honest day's pay. I don't feel like if I have to run out of the office, I am not taking anything away from anybody because I know I am going to get the job done. I think ultimately at the end of the day, that is what makes me feel right.

Ama has worked at two large law firms and two large corporations. In reflecting on her experiences, she has concluded that her fulfillment at each place of work came down to individual relationships, more so than the organizations. However, she is able to draw some conclusions on law firm life versus the corporate world.

Companies really do focus resources and energy on recognizing that a pleasant workplace means that you can retain a workforce. If you can retain a workforce, there is money that you save. There is a benefit to the corporation. There is a bottom line benefit in dollars and cents that companies have seen and recognized. Partly because there are more women in leadership roles than in traditional law firms. The conversation is changing so that there is a more open focus on healthy workplaces. On the law firm level, you don't see it in the same way.

Corporations may be more forward thinking in terms of setting up a healthy workplace that allows for balance. In Ama's opinion, law firms may fear becoming cutting edge in this respect. She notes of the Best Places to Work list, only one or two law firms make it onto the list each year, which is inconsequential to the number of corporations on such a list. In her words, "Corporations put a lot of energy into making the workplace right. There is a certain healthy competition among companies to do that."

Trying to achieve balance is Ama's greatest challenge. Sometimes this means just finding peace with the way things are and accepting that some things will have to be good enough and not be perfect.

Sometimes she does feel like she is shortchanging her kids, especially because of the nonstop world of technology. She wants to be more disciplined about putting her Blackberry away and being more present with them, but notes,

> If I am present with them, even if I am working, I feel better. I feel like it is not as if they are not seeing me. It is never going to be perfect.

At this point, she can discuss the kinds of sacrifices she needs to make with her kids. The fact that she is working might translate into a video game for her son, or the ability for the family to take a vacation. She notes that her greatest sacrifices have been in taking care of herself. She has a job where she is focused professionally, she is holding things together for her kids, but there is very little time for her to get to the gym or take care of her own needs. Relating to other moms, she notes, "We finish last. I put myself last a lot."

However, Ama lives without regret. Reflecting on motherhood and her career, she comments, "You have to be true to yourself. You have to do what feels good in your gut. . . . There are tradeoffs for every decision we make." Historically, the legal field has not been welcoming to mothers; therefore, in Ama's opinion it is important that women stay in the game. She also thinks there may be a shift as we currently have a generation of fathers who are more involved with their children.

The law can be an unrelenting and unforgiving profession; however, Ama is at a stage in her career where she has invested a lot, and she wants to see her work come to fruition. She laments the fact that so many women leave the profession:

> The reason that women opt out of practicing law when they are mothers has less to do with the fact that they are mothers, and more to do with the fact that they are feeling not so great about the profession. If you were feeling good about what you were doing and you were feeling like you could be successful or saw a path to success, I think you would have more reasons to stay and more reasons to make it work.

Interestingly, Ama would prefer her daughter not to follow her footsteps into a legal career. She would like her to be more aware of and open to professions that are more flexible. Perhaps if she does, in the future it will be a profession that has better adapted to the needs of working parents because of the work of Ama Romaine and other legal moms.

Chapter Eight

LEGAL MOM IN THE SILICON VALLEY

"Listen to your inner voice. Make it work.
Ask for what you need."
—Barbara Rogan

BARBARA ROGAN'S SOLE FOCUS in attending law school was to become a prosecutor. In high school, she became involved in speech and debate and watched episodes of *Law and Order*, fueling her dream.

Barbara attended Claremont McKenna College in Southern California, a liberal arts school focused on business and public affairs. Thereafter, she went to University of California Hastings College of Law. While in law school, Barbara took every course possible that would prepare her for a career as a prosecutor. She interned in the U.S. Attorney's Office and various District Attorneys offices. After law school, she got a job as an L.A. County Prosecutor, eventually moving to the Santa Clara County District Attorney's Office in order to live in the area where she grew up. Her move north was a conscious decision to live closer to the area where she ultimately wanted to raise a family.

After working for a time in the Santa Clara District Attorney's Office, Barbara began to look around in the technology industry. The year 2000 was the height of the tech boom, and there were terrific opportunities in technology law, despite her lack of experience in the field. She was able to secure an in-house job with a technology company but soon discovered that she had not taken any relevant classes to the field. She decided to return to school at Santa Clara University Law School to get an LL.M. in Intellectual Property Law. This additional degree gave her the knowledge in corporate and intellectual property law to make the transition.

After working as in-house counsel for two years, Barbara became pregnant and had her first child. Her daughter arrived two weeks early, and originally things went smoothly. Barbara took a full four months off. In California she was able to take four weeks of disability and an additional twelve weeks of FMLA leave. Her month of disability was paid, as was six weeks of her FMLA leave. Workers in California pay into the system in order to get these benefits. Barbara would have also been eligible to take another four weeks of disability before her daughter was born. Her company actually did not offer any maternity benefits because she was covered by the California state system.

After a few weeks her daughter began crying all the time, and on a gut level Barbara knew something was wrong. This part of the transition to motherhood was hard:

> I was trying to learn how to manage this child, knowing that something was wrong with her and that she was ill. And trying to just get through the day, because she pretty much cried unless she was asleep or eating. It was hard.

When Barbara went back to work, her daughter attended a full-time daycare and seemed to do fine. After dealing with her daughter's constant crying, the first couple of weeks back to work were a relief. They soon learned that her daughter had severe acid reflux and a bladder condition that caused infections in her bloodstream. Her daughter would routinely get very high fevers quickly and be put on antibiotic dosages. She eventually had corrective surgery.

Though she was working full time, Barbara serviced clients on the East Coast, so she was able to leave the office at 3:00 p.m. and then log back on in the evening. She also used technology—Blackberries, IMing, etc.—to keep in touch.

> Advice: Be flexible, because what you think might work out, doesn't always work out.

Now a mother of two daughters, over the years Barbara has utilized a variety of child care options, including full-time daycare, family members, part-time schedules, and most recently, her husband stays at home with her girls. In her words, "To think that you are going to have one childcare arrangement is not the case. I have had a lot of different childcare arrangements for different times in my life." She advises women to think early about what type of childcare arrangement will work because finding the right spot is critical:

Think about it early in your pregnancy. I got on wait lists when I was three months pregnant. . . . I got into all the daycares that I wanted because I thought about it so much in advance. I would have multiple options. I wouldn't just find one place and hope that it would work. I would recommend finding two or three places that would be okay with you and having them as options. It's better to say no to an option than to be struggling at the last minute to find something. . . . Do the due diligence. Give yourself plenty of time. Think about having a couple of different options. Don't just put all of your eggs in one basket.

She also credits having a wonderful partnership with her husband. Barbara's husband is a stay-at-home dad at this point. After the birth of her second child, Barbara chose to work part-time. However, the company for which she worked was purchased, and the new company asked her to move to San Diego. She decided to look for other options, but of the seven job offers she received, all of them were full time. Her husband was getting ready to begin law school, so they decided that he would be a stay-at-home dad as he made a career transition. This arrangement allowed Barbara to take a full-time job that was more intense than she had been able to take in the past. Initially, she was putting in ten-to-fourteen-hour days as she grew into her new role.

Although Barbara was able to focus more on her career, there were trade-offs in their new arrangement. She was used to running her kids' lives and has had to take a step back. During the first year, she had trouble handing off what they ate and planning their activities. At one point, she remarked, "Well, I don't even feel like I am a mother anymore." In addition, both she and her husband were sometimes jealous of the other: She envied his time with the girls; he envied that she spent time with adults. They were able to work through a compromise. Certain items were within her domain, including clothing and birthday gift purchases. She learned to let go of the other stuff. She describes this period:

> It was really hard. . . . I didn't feel like I was connected to them at all. I always felt like I was this person that happens to live in their house and donate money to their upkeep and am not their mother. . . . I didn't feel like a mother for maybe the first year.

As her husband started law school and her work schedule leveled off, she stopped feeling so disconnected.

Advice: Seek out other legal moms.

Barbara suggests reaching out to other moms to bounce ideas off each other and hear their struggles. "It is hard to be a parent, but is harder to be a mom because of the expectations that people put on moms." She thinks it is important to cultivate relationships with other legal moms, whether through law school connections or bar associations, because working in the law as a mom is a unique experience.

> In my experience, moms who happen to be lawyers tend to continue to work more than maybe moms who used to be marketing, for example, or who used to be in HR. They tend to stay with their career more than other types of professions. I think it is difficult because the expectation of the amount of work and availability that you are supposed to provide as a lawyer is different than in other groups. . . . Working in a corporation, they expect you to be available. . . . They are not going to be happy if a deal is delayed a couple of hours because you were off doing something. They expect you to respond.

Looking back, when she returned to work after having her first child, Barbara struggled with the perception that she wasn't as available or working as hard, but she learned that communication was essential. She concluded that her coworkers needed to know when she could complete a particular task. Her combination of excellent communication (returning calls and e-mails quickly) and meeting deadlines allowed her to beat the perception.

> Set your expectations. There are times when you have to do something immediately. It is maybe 5–10 percent of the time. The rest of the time you can negotiate and say, "Okay, I will have this to you, but it will be at 10:00 tonight," or "I will have this to you, but it is going to have to be tomorrow. Does that work for your timeframe?" . . . I try really hard not to say, "I can't do it because of my kids." I don't give a reason. I just say, "I can do it for you at this time. Does this work for you?" That way, I am not apologizing. It doesn't look like I am making excuses for my kids or my kids are interfering with my work.

In her opinion, over-sharing personal information can be a pitfall for working women. Barbara keeps her personal life out of the office. Rather than making explanations and apologies, giving a time frame is an effective tactic.

She continues to feel conflicted over her dual roles as an attorney and a mother. Barbara wants to be with her daughters to make memories but also wants to make sure she is doing a good job at work. She recently dealt with a situation where a board of directors meeting at her company was scheduled at the same time as her daughter's field trip. She describes this struggle:

> [There was] the immediacy of the need versus the long-term memories that I know would be more important. Ten years from now, am I even going to remember why I couldn't go, or what the board meeting was, or why I couldn't be there? No. Had I gone on the field trip with her, it would have been something special and something she really wanted me to do.

Barbara's ability to balance work and home life does allow her to step out of the office at times, for example to attend her youngest daughter's last day of preschool. However, she notes that balancing both roles is her biggest challenge. The competing desires in her life—doing a great job at work and being a terrific parent—leave her not always knowing whether she is succeeding at both.

Because of her split focus between work and family, Barbara sometimes feels like she is shortchanging herself. "What time I don't spend at work, I spend with my family." She spends a lot of time and energy making sure her kids are doing well. By putting her children and career first, she has not been able to devote time to friendships that other women seem to have who do not have children or moms that stay at home . She sees the friendships that stay-at-home moms in her neighborhood have, but she isn't able to devote the same time or attention to maintaining such ties.

Barbara has also sacrificed career opportunities in the name of her family. When her oldest daughter was dealing with medical issues, Barbara was plucked for an intense job that would have required more hours and an increased commitment. She chose not to pursue it, knowing that there are times in life for some things, and times for other things.

> In looking back at those decisions, I made the decision that was right for her and for me because my heart would have been broken if I hadn't been able to be there for her.

Barbara made a series of choices to provide her children with the childhood that she had—wonderful schools and a great community. Choosing to relocate to Silicon Valley, choosing to work in-house, and choosing to work a part-time schedule for a time, enhanced her ability to be the parent she wants to be.

Advice: Ask for what you need. Don't apologize.

Barbara's employers have all been supportive. However, working in the tech industry in Silicon Valley, she notes that young men have traditionally staffed the industry. This has lent itself to a culture of working 24/7/365, with the company providing free meals, free coffee, workout facilities, and ping-pong. This culture allows employees to talk about work nonstop, with one's whole life revolving around technology. This type of workplace does not work very well from a mother's perspective, as many moms prefer to be at home with their family at a reasonable time. This culture was hard for Barbara at first because she was, in some respects, bucking the culture. She deals with it by knowing,

> If you are a good employee and you do good work and you get your work done and you are available . . . then you can get away with not having to spend twelve to fourteen hours at work.

She minimizes her discussion about her children in the workplace but has her daughters' artwork everywhere in her office. Barbara manages expectations properly in order to deal with any "mommy stigma." When requesting time off or dealing with her schedule, she emphasizes her work, rather than her role as a mom.

> I do strongly feel that there is a huge bias if you as a woman talk too much about your kids and your needs; you are going to be perceived as not working as hard.

If women are willing to ask for what they need, Barbara thinks that the law can be a great career for women, particularly because it affords so many choices. She cautions women not to count themselves out career-wise because of the desire to raise children: "We constantly are down-selecting our careers. . . . To some extent, we have to speak up and articulate what we need, even if it isn't standard."

Barbara attributes her own success to hard work *and* the fact that she has invested in the development of her career. In switching practice areas from criminal to corporate and intellectual property, she pursued additional education and sought opportunities that would develop her skills.

> As a lawyer, you have to develop yourself constantly because this is a constantly changing world. The skills sets that make you valuable to a law firm or a company, they change. If you don't change, you are going to be out of a job.

As she has developed within her practice area, Barbara has continued to enjoy her job, particularly the combination of business and law. Although she isn't sure of what the future holds, she can reflect on raising her daughters and notice that things have gotten a little easier over the years.

Particularly, she can reflect on her own choices and offer the following advice: "Do what is right for your family and don't judge yourself so much."

Part Three

WORKING FOR UNCLE SAM

Chapter Nine

DISCOVERING THE GOVERNMENT: STEERING A COURSE OUT OF LAW FIRM LIFE

"The coolest part about being a mom is the opportunity to rediscover everything in the world."
—*Maggie Harris*

MAGGIE HARRIS DESCRIBES HERSELF as an oldest child who was very pragmatic and focused. She was someone who strived to "be good" and "make people happy." As a junior high and high school student, Maggie completed her parents' tax returns for fun. She was always a strong student. In high school, she decided that she would either pursue a career in accountancy or the law. Her father had worked in sales, dealing with the uncertainty of the market. Maggie wanted a career that would engage her intellect, yet provide a stable career trajectory and paycheck.

As an undergraduate Political Science student at Emory University in Atlanta, Maggie worked part time in the General Counsel's office. The job was fascinating—one day the office would be preparing contracts for a music group to play on campus, while the next day they would be reviewing construction contracts. As she was making the decision where to attend law school, the General Counsel for Emory, advised her that choosing the best school would pay dividends throughout her career because her resume would rise to the top of the pile. She chose to attend Harvard Law School, despite earning a full scholarship to University of Notre Dame. She feels that her choice to attend Harvard has given her more opportunities and allowed her more flexibility in her career because she has an extraordinary credential.

Maggie enjoyed Harvard but missed the intellectual stimulation she found in Political Science. She felt that many of the Harvard Law professors were pursuing their own practice or research agendas at the expense of their classroom obligations. However, Maggie found particular inspiration from some of her professors, notably Laurence Lessig.

Despite being in a serious relationship, Maggie admits that during law school, she gave little thought to what her life might be like beyond her legal career. Marriage, kids, and so forth were a "someday" thought. She focused on her schoolwork and finding a good position after graduation. She now remarks:

> I think it is a wonderful thing that girls and women are encouraged by their families to pursue professional degrees and go for it 100 percent, but no one ever talks to you about the great sacrifices you will have to make, the extraordinary juggling, or the things you are going to have to cope with down the road.

Maggie spent her second summer splitting her time between two large DC law firms: one based in New York City, one based in Atlanta. She ultimately chose to begin her career in the Washington, DC office of the Atlanta-based firm. She thought the culture of the firm was slightly less stressful, and she was particularly drawn to the international tax work that they were doing. During her first and second year at the firm, Maggie focused on working hard and making her billable hour requirement; however, she began to notice that most of the female partners were either unmarried or childless. Most of the male partners had stay-at-home wives that handled their home life. She started to think about how long she might be able to sustain the pressure of law firm work and realized early that with or without a family, it was not a life that she would ultimately be happy living.

After being at the firm for two years, Maggie got married and started to think about her next career move. She saw her firm colleagues a year or two ahead of her moving toward partnership and their grind did not appeal to her. She felt that pursuing partnership was a very black or white thing—if she was to go for partnership, her whole life was going to be the firm, to the detriment of her personal life.

> At the time there was a real acknowledgment that firms and companies were not dealing well—they were losing very educated women because they were not being very flexible about these matters. It seemed like it was becoming a cachet thing for firms to say they were concerned about work-life balance. My firm was leading in work-life balance numbers, and yet to be successful there and to feel successful, there was really not any sort of work-life balance.

Maggie started to think about other options. Being in Washington, DC, she thought government work would provide the best of both worlds—stimulating work with better work-life balance. During her third year at the firm, she concluded that she most wanted to work in the General Counsel's office of the IRS. Unfortunately, lateral hires were rare. She spent another year at her firm waiting for a position to become available. Maggie comments about her reasons for pursuing a job with the federal government:

> In my view, with the IRS, especially the Counsel's office, we have a lot of great female attorneys who have left law firms and come to the government. I think it is because it is one of the only places that allow the flexibility and a little more of the regularity that you need to have some sort of home life.

Once settled into a stable government job, Maggie became pregnant. She worried about what other people in the office would think about her starting a job, then starting a family. Some colleagues commented that she probably wouldn't come back to work after having the baby. Maggie was resolute—she knew that she wanted to be a working mom.

Maggie has thought about what it might be like to stay home with her daughter. However, she craves the intellectual stimulation that work provides. Her mother had been a working mother, who had spent every ounce of energy and time outside of work raising her children. Maggie learned that by being happy and engaged at work, she would project a positive image to her daughter. She also feels like she spends a tremendous amount of time, energy, and focus on her daughter when she is not working.

Maggie's daughter, Genevieve, was born in 2007. She is a tremendous joy to both of her parents. Interestingly, Maggie did not have "maternity leave" working for the government. Under the Family Medical Leave Act, she was able to take six weeks off; however, she needed to use the paid time off she had accrued. She ultimately took five weeks off, and her husband, a college professor who was off for the summer, took over until he was back at work.

As a young family in Washington, DC, with two working parents, their toughest challenge initially was securing daycare. When Maggie was three months pregnant, they put their names on twelve daycare waiting lists. Nearly a year later, spots had opened up in only two centers. Maggie struggled to make sure that she picked up Genevieve on time and tried to balance her demanding career with raising an infant daughter.

As they adjusted to parenthood, Maggie's husband was offered a faculty position near Buffalo, New York. It was clearly a great opportunity for him, but they struggled with how it would affect Maggie's career. The move may not have made sense on paper or to Maggie's colleagues in the law. As a family, they chose to prioritize her husband's career in academia that was not as lucrative as the law. The IRS General Counsel's Office did not have an opportunity for her in Buffalo, and she was unable to receive a "hardship transfer." Initially, Maggie remained in DC on her own, juggling work and her daughter on her own.

Eventually Maggie was able to secure a position with the IRS Appeals Division working out of Buffalo. She believes that the IRS was very good about valuing her for what she brought to the table and did not look strictly at geographical limitations. She has been able to rise within the organization and has not necessarily been limited by living in a smaller legal market.

The move to Buffalo was ultimately a great move for them as a family. In a smaller city, they began to explore the area's family-friendly attractions—sledding, skiing, apple picking, and visiting local farms. Their commutes became more predictable and manageable. Maggie also found that the innate friendliness of the people created a terrific support system for her, as her own family lived mostly in the Atlanta area.

Looking back at her career choices, Maggie would advise her younger self to give more serious consideration to living near family and extended family. This was not necessarily a factor when she was in the initial interview process during law school, but she recognizes the importance of additional support now that she has her own family.

> At Harvard, you have all these top firms courting you. I think it is really hard when you are twenty-five years old to make sacrifices in your career when you haven't started seriously thinking seriously about work-life balance.

Without extended family support, Maggie has found that the biggest sacrifice she has made as a working mother is losing her "me" time. Because her time with Genevieve is limited during the week, she tries to be completely present in the evenings and on weekends. This means that she often loses out on working out and pursuing things she might otherwise enjoy—cultural attractions particularly. In describing this lack of "me" time, she comments:

> The loss of autonomy and time and energy for yourself and your own interests [is difficult]. It seems like 98 percent of my time and energy is work or childrearing. I am always trying to balance time between those two things. . . . You start to feel like there is nothing that is just yours. I find that more with me and my female friends than with our husbands. I feel guilty about anything that is not geared toward work or my daughter.

Maggie has worked to get herself into a position that she can be involved in her daughter's day-to-day life. However, she and her husband are constantly balancing responsibilities because Maggie travels for work, and his position has additional responsibilities related to research and publishing. Juggling such responsibilities is akin to "passing the baton" in a relay race. At this point, their careers are balanced in the sense that they are able to juggle the demands; however, they have set up their lives to allow for such pursuits.

Advice: Finding the right childcare situation makes all the difference.

Genevieve is in full-time daycare, five days per week. After having such difficulty finding childcare in the DC area, Maggie was thrilled to find a terrific NAYEC certified daycare in their area of Buffalo. She thinks the arrangement has worked well for their work schedules and is the optimal environment for her daughter.

> I feel like daycare is really good for her because she has a cadre of friends. She is into the structured environment. She gets so much out of it that I can't imagine her not being in that environment.

At home, Maggie doesn't think she would be able to fill the time in the same engaging way that the daycare offers. In addition, the daycare has become a terrific support system for their family. One particular evening, Maggie was travelling and her husband was delayed picking up Genevieve due to weather conditions. One of the teachers at the daycare who had a car seat was able to bring Genevieve home to their house and babysit for a couple of hours until he could get home. Maggie really feels that there is a kindness in her community that supports them as a young family with two working parents.

Despite having terrific childcare arrangements, Maggie still battles some of the guilt that many working mothers feel. She mentions that recently a colleague brought a newspaper clipping into work indicating that mothers, both stay-at-home and working women, spend more time with their children now than the typical traditional stay-at-home mom did in the idealized 1950s and 1960s. Maggie describes past decades as a time with different child and adult spheres—adults were not necessarily as intimately involved in their children's lives.

Advice: Take time to enjoy the little things.

Maggie is in a transition now as her daughter emerges from toddlerhood. She is questioning how to model the behavior of caring for her child along with caring for herself and avoiding the traps of helicopter parenting. Her delight in parenting and having time to spend with her daughter are evident.

> It really gets me back to so many things that I had pushed to the side and out of my mind because I was so focused on career and work— whether it is nature hikes or other things in life that had been whirl-

ing past. Genevieve can really focus on a caterpillar or some little thing that I wouldn't have even stopped to look at. The coolest part about being a mom is the opportunity to rediscover everything in the world.

Enjoying childlike activities is a good way for Maggie to put the demands of the legal profession into perspective. She has been able to carve out this time because she thought carefully about how she could ascend within the law and have a reasonable schedule that would support raising a child. Maggie feels that the government is a supportive employer, particularly the IRS. It not only promotes work-life balance but also allows for a more regular schedule. In addition, there are certain benefits built into the government system such as flexible work hours and the ability to work from home.

For Maggie, satisfaction with her work environment comes down to the people with whom she works. Many of them have made the decision to work in the government, despite having a lucrative career in the private sector. The general attitude of her colleagues is that Maggie is working at a high level, and if she does an outstanding job, they are not concerned about "face-time" that would be more important in firm culture.

Despite the flexibility her job allows, Maggie is not living in a perfect world. Her job requires travel, which she attempts to minimize by taking early flights out of town and late flights into town. She also makes an effort to bring Genevieve with her on longer trips in cities where she has family that can help.

Maggie describes the legal profession as ultimately a service-oriented job. The impact of parenthood to women in the profession may come down to a question of commitment to the demands of the law: Are you available at any time? Are you going to be there when you are needed? Are you providing 100 percent service? In order to keep mothers involved in the profession with some level of sanity, the nature of the profession is in question:

> It would require significant flexibility on the part of clients and the existing management and partners of firms. . . . How do you balance the demands of a service profession with these other extended family needs? . . . Law firms and companies recognize it, and they try to put some window-dressing on it with family-friendly type policies. From

what I have seen, at the end of the day, the work and the nature of the work is driving this need to have people that are fully committed to the cause.

The demands of her career have made her question whether having more children would be feasible. Maggie is concerned that having a second child may require additional sacrifices, and her career may need to move to the sidelines. On a long-term basis, she is not sure whether that would satisfy her. She feels like she has moved her career to the flexible limit. Even though she has a flexible work environment, she is still on a career track with the IRS. Having a second child might impede her career development.

> Advice: Think carefully about work-life issues early in your career.

If she could have a conversation with her law school self, Maggie would emphasize that there are very different law practices that have different demands in terms of their scheduling. To have a blended life, women really need to think seriously on the front end. There are a lot more opportunities for flexibility in certain types of legal careers. Identifying these practice areas early can avoid issues later.

Additionally, had she known what she wanted sooner and understood her life goals, she would have tried to go to the government sooner, despite the lower pay scale as compared to private practice. She would have had the ability to rise within the ranks before taking on the responsibility of motherhood.

Chapter Ten

THE GUILT-FREE LEGAL MOM: NOT AN OXYMORON

"Learn to let go of the guilt. When you are away from your kids, you try to be the best lawyer you can be. When you are with your kids, try to be the best mother you can be."
—Tara Ori

As a mother of three children under the age of seven, working full time in the Civil Division of the State Attorney's Office north of Chicago, Tara Ori is no stranger to hard work. Despite pursuing a career in the legal field, Tara knew that she wanted a family and was willing to make the sacrifices necessary to make her career and family life work.

As an undergraduate at Northwestern University, Tara majored in Social Policy with a concentration in History and Psychology, knowing that she would likely pursue law school. However, she wasn't so sure if she wanted a career as a practicing lawyer. Upon graduation, she worked for a few months as a temp in some law offices and ultimately made the decision to enroll at John Marshall Law School in Chicago beginning in their January term 2001.

Not only did Tara earn her JD, she also found the love of her life in law school. She was married in November of her final year to a law school classmate. They were able to study and take the Illinois Bar Exam together. After receiving her law license in May of 2004, Tara began practicing for a boutique Insurance Defense firm in downtown Chicago. Her husband had accepted a job in the suburbs as an assistant state's attorney.

They always knew that they wanted to have a family, which Tara credits partially to their Catholic faith. Although they made a deal to wait to have children until she had worked for a while, simultaneously they made the decision to move to the suburbs knowing it was ultimately where they wanted to be when the kids arrived.

In October, Tara discovered she was pregnant, approximately three months after starting her first job. Around that time, she also started to look for a new job, wanting to work closer to home and to her husband's work, knowing there would be childcare concerns on the horizon.

Tara began the job search process in earnest as a soon-to-be mother. In April, she secured an interview with the States Attorney's Office where her husband worked, but in the Civil Division. She could not conceal the pregnancy, as she was due just two months later, and her husband had already disclosed within the office that they were expecting.

Although the interviewers asked all of the standard questions during the interview, they did not broach the subject of her pregnancy. Tara decided to lay it out there, knowing that they were aware of her circumstances. Rather than dancing around the subject, she was direct:

> I know you know I am pregnant. Of course, I am going to take a maternity leave. I don't know how long yet. . . . I do of course plan on coming back . . . full time.

To her relief, they related that one of the attorneys in the office was actually on maternity leave. What could have or should have been an awkward moment turned into a very comfortable situation. Tara was nervous but also was able to emphasize that she really wanted the job.

Tara was hired and still appreciates that the office was willing to take a chance on her, knowing that there was a possibility she would change her mind and not return after her maternity leave. She was able to work from the beginning of April until nearly her due date of June 26. It helped that the person Tara was replacing had not been working at full capacity because of a medical issue; therefore, she was not filling an immediate void.

Tara took eight weeks off after her oldest child was born. As she was the first one of her friends to have a baby, she really didn't know what to expect, especially in regard to returning to work. No one she knew continued working after having a baby. Without having a confidant in this regard, she was unsure about her new role.

On her first day back to the office, Tara says that she "cried the entire day." Overall, it took a week or two to get into a good routine. It certainly helped that both she and her husband worked in the same office. They were able to drive together, sharing drop-off and pick-up duties at the home-based daycare that they chose.

> Advice: Find childcare early.

As she went into labor three weeks early, Tara and her husband were not completely ready with their daycare arrangements. She did further research during her maternity leave, and two weeks before she came back to work, Tara found a friend's aunt who provided in-home daycare that would consist of her daughter and one other child. They felt very comfortable with the situation; however, they had initially considered only traditional daycare settings. Their daughter stayed with this first care provider until she was six months old. At that time, Tara discovered a new sitter providing care in her home, and six years later she now sends all three children there.

With her children aged six, four and three, Tara has a lot on her plate right now. She comments, "I am either lawyer or mom-wife. I have little kid stuff going on all the time." Despite what she had earlier pictured, juggling both worlds has become harder as the kids have gotten older because they have their own schedules and extra curricular activities. She notes, "I have to be way more organized than I had to be when they were babies."

Tara tries to carve out time to be involved in the children's daily school lives. As long as she can schedule events far in advance, she will get to the school as she can. If she isn't able to do so, she simply lets it go—avoiding the guilt that many mothers carry. At least once a month, she takes a longer lunch and goes to the playground to see the kids at school. Because her office is forty minutes from the school, it can make it difficult in traffic, but Tara does her best to make it work. She also credits her husband's support in helping her manage everything. As he now has his own law firm, his schedule is often more flexible.

Many mothers feel pangs of stress and guilt when they are not always able to be there for their kids. Although Tara certainly gives her kids her all, it is interesting that she didn't have the sometimes-overwhelming feelings of guilt that many mothers describe. She notes that keeping busy has been a positive strategy for letting go of guilt:

> I am way too busy to feel as guilty as I was when I was a new mom. I have more cases and more responsibility as I have grown as an attorney, so I really don't have the time that I used to when I first came back with my son.

Because she wasn't yet working at full capacity when she began her job, she had a lot of time to think about being away from her newborn son initially. These feelings have subsided over the years:

> After three [children], everybody is fine. I am sure I have missed important things, but I think that with experience . . . you learn that everything is going to be fine. . . . It is easier to let go with experience and with age.

As Tara had her son when she was 27, she really didn't know what to expect, commenting, "I didn't have a lot of working mom role models to sort of play off of." Her maturation process as both an attorney and as a mother has allowed her to let go of the idea of perfection and enjoy both roles simultaneously.

Tara credits her husband with being a good balance for her and incredibly supportive. In her words, "He recognizes that I work as much as he does, so it has to be 50/50 or it is not going to work." In addition, Tara's mother now lives with her family. Her mom picks kids up from school and helps to shuttle them to extracurricular activities. Neighbors and other school parents act as a backup as well. Tara feels like they have hit their stride as a family, noting, "I am feel like I am coming up for air where I was drowning a couple of years ago."

Advice: Sometimes the passage of time helps shape a new perspective.

As she reflects on her career at this point, Tara remembers second-guessing her decision to pursue a career in the law when she was initially practicing, saying, "I kind of always said, 'Why did I do this? Why did I take out all these loans?'" Now she is glad that she persevered, as the kids are getting older and are more independent. She didn't feel this way when they were babies. She has also accepted certain limitations. She relates, "I can't do it all. I definitely know that, but I am doing something with this education and the opportunities that I have been given. I don't second-guess it now, but I did when I was younger."

It has helped that her workplace has been supportive. She has been able to take extra time as needed—when the kids are sick, and so forth. She also does not have the billable hour requirement that many of her law school colleagues have at firms, and she can generally shut off any work-related concerns after 5:00 p.m., spending the evening at soccer or making dinner. Tara also feels fortunate that all of her immediate coworkers are parents and they understand parenting issues. The workplace culture is family friendly where colleagues feel comfortable displaying pictures of their children and their children's artwork.

As a government employee, Tara also enjoys predictability and a stable paycheck. Her hours are generally 8:00 a.m. to 5:00 p.m. Although she may make half of what a private attorney makes, the fact that her office has not seen the mass layoffs that many law firms have seen in the economic downturn is comforting.

Tara does note that unlike some law offices, as a government attorney, she does not have the luxury of working from home or flextime. These are perks that she would have appreciated when her children were very young. As she never had that option, she dealt with it. Tara has never had any negative experiences related to her role as a mother in the small legal community in which she works. She has never felt that she was perceived as weak or incapable because she has three children.

In watching her friends at big law firms, Tara has the general impression that big law firms are not a supportive environment. From what she has heard, women know at the outset that partnership track will not be an option should they choose to have children and deviate from the standard law firm trajectory. For the most part, Tara's law school classmates continue to work in the legal field; however, she feels that it is probably not always a choice but may be based on law school loans.

Tara had to navigate the waters of working parenthood on her own in the sense that she did not have any mentors or know anyone in the same situation. Some of her coworkers have older children, but when she had small babies at home, Tara didn't know anyone who could immediately relate to her situation. Because the parents in the office have children in all age ranges, it has actually been helpful to her as Tara navigates how to deal with school issues—she can see the road before her.

At this point, Tara's children seem to have a positive impression of her career. They have been used to being cared for by others in addition to their parents from a very young age and have adapted to their routine well. Tara used to feel that she might be shortchanging her kids by working; however, she now comments,

> After number one, I realized that you don't need to spend 24 hours a day with them. . . . For the most part, I am not shortchanging them. I am there and I am able to see that now three kids later. With my first, I did feel that I was missing out.

In addition to her career and family, Tara takes time to foster her own personal health and wellness. She always makes sure she has time to run each day, even waking up sometimes at 4:00 a.m. to make sure that it happens. Her kids see her exercise and know that it makes her feel great. She comments, "I am a bad mother. I am a bad wife. I am a bad attorney, if I don't have that time for myself." As a mom, Tara has become more serious about running. She has trained for a marathon, regularly taking on 20-mile weekend runs. Her family has been very supportive. They know how important running is to her.

At this point, both her personal life and career are running smoothly. Ultimately, Tara would like to continue working for the government but dreams of transitioning into the judiciary at some point. As they are rooted in the area, Tara has volunteered to serve on bar association committees. She is willing to the put in the time, partially because of her career aspirations. Her husband is on board with these goals, and they are fortunate to have her mother as an additional support should Tara or her husband pursue a judicial position in the future.

Perhaps it is motherhood, perhaps age, or perhaps experience, but Tara does not find herself stressing out about things as much as she has in the past, both in the workplace or at home. As many attorneys exhibit a type-A personality, Tara's approach seems unique:

I have learned to let go of being absolutely perfect with everything that I write or do or speak at work because this isn't law school. . . . If I have a ton of briefs due, it is going to be okay; it may not be the most perfect document, but it will get done.

Similarly in her personal life, Tara has learned to reach out to others and no longer feels the need to have complete control over the home front. If a grandparent volunteers to take the kids for a weekend, she is willing to accept the help and not worry whether they serve green beans and the kids don't like it.

> ### Advice: Let go of mommy guilt.

Tara advises other women to take a similar approach, relaxing their own standards of perfection. She advises not stressing over guilt, being honest with priorities as a mom, and accepting what you can and cannot do. With the added responsibilities of motherhood, no one can be all things to all people:

Learn to let go of the guilt. When you are away from your kids, you try to be the best lawyer you can be. When you are with your kids, try to be the best mother you can be. You have to let go of that guilt. You have to be sort of honest about what you are able to do. When taking on extra responsibilities, you have to be very honest with yourself. I am not going to be able to do everything because I am a mother, and that is hard to grasp until you are actually there.

> ### Advice: Docket your personal life.

Tara also shares a few tried and true strategies that her family has employed to handle things on the home front. They have found that having professional cleaners has been worth the extra expense with two working parents. As Tara and her husband share the household duties 50/50, it also helps to separate tasks; for example, she does the laundry and he does the dishes.

Tara and her husband also utilize Google extensively to manage their personal lives. They use Gmail and Google Calendar to coordinate schedules. If she knows that she will need to be in federal court, she will send her husband a meeting request notifying him of any transferred responsibilities. Similarly, he lets her know via Gmail and the appointment function whether he has late appointments on a given night. Tara comments, "We are not the most organized people in the world, but we do need to make sure people are where they are supposed to be."

Tara enjoys her job as an attorney and comes to the conclusion that it is a good job for a mom. There is flexibility within the profession, and she is developing a marketable skill that could apply to several different professions should her job ever be in jeopardy.

She also takes great pride and enjoyment in her children. As they grow up, she sees more in common with other mothers, both working moms and stay-at-home moms. There is really one common goal: raising well-adjusted happy children. Tara's balanced life seems to be on track for this purpose:

> I couldn't imagine my life without my kids. It is just so gratifying teaching these three little people everything that I know and having funny little conversations with them. . . . I could never imagine not having them. It is hard for me to even remember how we were before having them.

Note:

Mama Law—
The Power of Friendship

THE NEXT TWO CHAPTERS PROFILE STACEY FERGUSON and Nadia Jones, respectively. They have chosen to share their stories as legal moms and as a testament to their enduring friendship through the challenges of career and children. Stacey Ferguson is a government attorney specializing in media law. Nadia Jones is an Assistant Professor of Lawyering Skills at Florida Coastal School of Law. Along with another law school classmate, they cofounded www.mamalaw.com, a forum to discuss their experiences juggling family life with practicing law or as they describe it "evidence for our insanity plea."

Their initial blog began in 2006 when they were all dealing with issues related to raising young babies—sleeping through the night, breastfeeding, and so forth. The e-mails were flying fast and furious each day from all three of the women. After reading a parenting blog, Stacey thought that they could convert their e-mail discussion into a blog, bringing their experience to other women who might be struggling with similar issues.

As part of their blog, they created laws that would help moms navigate life—calling them Mama Laws. Some include "Respect the nap," "Stop and smell the dirty diapers," and "Don't worry, you'll figure it out." Mamalaw.com now has hundreds of followers reading posts on how to make it work.

The honesty of their posts is incredibly refreshing. Some topics include "File Me under the Worst Mom Ever" (for missing Muffins with Mom at school), "Free or Cheap Summer Fun for Kids" (ideas to keep the summer moving), and "Camp Torture" (a narrative of how much one of the children hated summer camp). The message from these posts is that none of us is alone in dealing with the curveballs thrown at us while raising kids.

In spring 2009, the women created a blogging conference focused specifically for multicultural bloggers, dubbed Blogalicious. Their first conference sold out at 175 attendees and welcomed huge corporate sponsors. They have built not only a website but also an online community. Their tagline is "To raise the visibility of women of color online and to celebrate diversity." In addition to their media work, they have thriving legal careers. How do they make it all work? Read on. . . .

Chapter Eleven

KNOWING WHAT YOU WANT IS HALF THE BATTLE

"Do your research. Look internally and decide what it is you think is most important to you."

—*Stacey Ferguson*

Stacey Ferguson majored in Communications at the University of Florida in Gainesville, with an emphasis on Television Production, and a minor in Criminal Justice. She wanted to have a career in media—her dream job was to be a producer for award shows.

However, in her junior year Stacey began investigating the salaries of entry-level production jobs and realized that she wanted more, so her Plan B became law school. She soon found that many people in law school were there because they also didn't know exactly what they wanted to do. Stacey chose to attend Howard University School of Law, where she had an excellent experience.

> I loved law school. I think it had a lot do with the particular school I attended. Howard was very much a family atmosphere, steeped in history, civil rights, and making social change. . . . The first week we

all had to go through orientation during which we watched *Eyes on the Prize*, the civil rights series. You got the feeling that you were in a different place because they wanted you to know where you were coming from, where you were going, and what kind of atmosphere you were coming into. . . .

At the end of the orientation, they said, "Look to your left, look to your right. At other law schools they say, one of those people won't be there when you graduate, but at Howard we say it is your job to make sure that both of those people are there with you." . . . It is really a testament to what the personality and character of the school was.

Based on her very positive law school experience, Stacey was excited about practicing law. She decided to pursue entertainment law, describing it as "cool and sexy." At Howard, she took Intellectual Property classes and became the president of the Sports and Entertainment Law Section. She chose to summer at an M100 law firm based in New York, working on great cases for celebrity clients such as Madonna, Shania Twain, Lauryn Hill, and the NBA. She even attended the NBA draft and the Tony awards.

However, after spending the summer in New York and receiving a job offer, Stacey decided it was just too big for her, and she asked if the firm's DC office had any entertainment law work. She was assured that they did, and she joined the firm after graduation in 2002.

Unfortunately, there was not quite enough entertainment work at the DC office, so Stacey learned corporate law, which was of great benefit to her: "At the end of the day, entertainment law is contracts and intellectual property." However, after a few months at the firm, she began to take on mostly litigation cases, many dealing with privacy issues.

During her time at the firm, she experienced a great deal of anxiety. The pressure of performing in a sometimes-hostile environment overwhelmed her:

The hours are hard. The respect you get as a junior associate is minimal. Literally being cursed at, screamed at, and always mistaken for the secretary because I am African American, and clearly they assumed I just couldn't be the attorney. . . . I would have panic attacks, I would be shaking, I would have headaches, I would be crying in the bathroom.

Stacey started seeing a therapist who prescribed her anxiety medication. In 2003, Stacey was married, and the following year she became pregnant with her first daughter. Stacey describes this as an "aha" moment: She thought to herself, "I am 27 years old, why am I taking anxiety medication?" Knowing the pressure she was under, Stacey didn't feel that working in litigation and having a small child would be a feasible schedule. The hours were both long and unpredictable.

> I remember being nine months pregnant and being at the office at 11:00 at night, and the partner looked at me and looked down at my stomach and asked, "Did you eat dinner?" . . . At that point, I thought, I have got to look for other options.

Once she became pregnant, she really began to think about her life at the firm, specifically as it related to her anxiety. She did not have a long-term goal of making partner, and she knew she did not want to be miserable. She thought:

> It doesn't have to be like this. I will be treated the way I let them treat me. It was really hard to come to that conclusion. Something definitely clicked. . . . I only have one life. I am having a baby. I should not be miserable every day. I put my foot down mentally. . . . I set up boundaries for myself. I wouldn't check my Blackberry after 10:00 p.m. and all weekend.
> You get brainwashed when you are at a firm. You think you always have to be on call and say yes to everything and be available to everyone and be available on the weekends. You actually don't, and people will figure it out. That clarity did not come until I was pregnant.

Stacey heard about an opening at a federal agency for an attorney with experience in privacy law, specifically spyware. She applied for the position but did not receive a call. So she decided to stay with the firm and be proactive about making her hours more reasonable. She approached the partners about joining the Health Care group, as she had transactional experience and she knew that it was a good group that had reasonable hours. The firm agreed.

Stacey relates that being a mother really "emboldens you." After joining the Health Care group, she then decided to also ask if she could go part time. The firm again agreed. She worked three days a week, Monday through Wednesday.

Stacey also joined the Working Parents Committee at her firm. One of the speakers who attended a meeting was a female partner from the New York office. She described how she achieved work-life balance. One of her solutions was to have her husband bring her children to the law firm cafeteria so that she could have dinner with her kids and then go back to work. This scenario did not appeal to Stacey, although she readily acknowledges that everyone is different in this respect.

After a year, she received a call from the federal agency and started with them in the summer of 2005 when she was four months pregnant with her second child. She describes it as an ideal situation:

> It is a very family friendly casual atmosphere. Great people. Great work. Everyone is understanding that you have a life outside of the office.

Ironically, although the government is a great place to work, they do not have a maternity leave policy, which really surprised Stacey. She was able to take only paid leave that she had accrued. Having started with the agency when she was four months pregnant, she was not eligible for paid leave. She took all of her sick and vacation time, which was two weeks. She put in a special request to her manager for two months unpaid.

> It is [Washington] DC, there are hundreds of thousands of people working in government—a lot of them women. How come nobody is picketing on the White House lawn for maternity leave? I don't get it.

In October of 2010, she decided to go to a part-time schedule. She had three children under the age of six, and with she and her husband working full time, Stacey felt that she needed to dial back her career. "It just got to be too much." In addition, her social media work with www.mamalaw.com was taking off considerably, including the creation of the Blogalicious conference. She now works four days a week, three days in the office and one at home. Although her schedule is more flexible, it is still quite demanding. "It is definitely still hard juggling because I never feel like I am 100 percent at home or at work."

One of the biggest regrets she has is not being home when her kids were young, but she really didn't think about being a stay-at-home mom before she had children. Her own mother always worked. It never occurred to at her to stay home until she had children.

In hindsight, I would have planned a little bit differently. . . . I really feel a huge sense of guilt and sadness at not being home with my kids. I felt a pull so strongly to stay home once I had kids, but it was too late. We had already a purchased a house that we had a mortgage on, and had cars that we had to pay on, and we live in an expensive area.

Her first daughter had four separate daycare/preschool programs before she was six. Stacey describes her as totally fine and well adjusted, but Stacey feels guilt about it. Her second daughter had a combination of daycare and a nanny. Stacey's son, her youngest child, has only been at home because they decided to employ a nanny during the last three years. Stacey describes finding a nanny as a very difficult process.

> Advice: Make a list of responsibilities at home and split them.

Stacey and her husband share childcare responsibilities. When they had their first child, he also worked a reduced schedule in order to cover childcare. As a software engineer, he loves what he does. She describes one of their secrets is to have very delineated responsibilities. As it seemed that they were often arguing over duties within the household, Stacey typed up a document listing each of their responsibilities and they discussed them. They developed a system that works, with specified responsibilities that do not cross over. She describes her husband as 50-50 on the parenting front.

Stacey would prefer to work on her budding media empire on a more full-time basis, but her government position gives her family the stability that she needs. She feels that it is important for women to know what they want and be clear about it. She gives the following advice:

Do your research. Look internally and decide what it is you think is most important to you. If you know that the money and making partner is more important to you, you'll be able to plan for that at the outset and come up with an arrangement that works. If you know that you want to stay home or work part time or have an alternative legal career, then figure that out at the outset, and that way you can plan for it better. . . . And speak about it with your spouse and the expectations that you have.

Stacey describes her experience of law firm culture as very male oriented, focused on money and work output. She believes there needs to be an acknowledgement that people working at firms are in fact PEOPLE, with personal lives. There needs to be flexible arrangements—working from home when possible and weekends should be off limits. There also needs to be an understanding that family responsibilities are important. At the firm where Stacey worked, all of the men were partners with wives at home. She relates, "They didn't have to worry about the concert, or the bake sale, or the book fair because they had someone at home taking care of it." With more female partners at law firms, Stacey feels that some of these issues might be addressed.

One universal solution that Stacey proposes to help working parents is that the workday match the school day. There is a huge disconnect between the workplace, school, and parenting. Her children's schools will invite her to a parent social at 2:00 in the afternoon, where she and the other working parents are nearly always put in a bind. It is as if the world has not caught on that most parents are both working full time, and that society has to address it.

> Advice: When times get tough, connect with friends.

Stacey acknowledges that she does still feel overwhelmed at times. When she had her third child last year, she thought she had everything under control. However, she soon realized that she had taken on too much—greater responsibilities at work and another child at home. During that time, she blogged about her feelings and had what she describes as a mini-breakdown. She got through it by connecting to her friends, bloggers, and by making some changes at work. When she went through her review, she answered the question "How are you doing?" with the response, "Honestly, I am falling apart." Her manager asked if Stacey had thought about reducing her hours, and ultimately worked with her to find a more manageable schedule.

At the end of the day, Stacey is grateful for the online community that she has built that helps her stay sane as she navigates her career and family life. Blogging has given her an outlet for her frustrations and connected her to friends she would not have otherwise had.

> You feel so connected, you are not alone. It is a great support system. It is like my moms' group, but times a thousand. . . . With this trend in the mom blogs, it has really empowered women. Those who were

at home, probably feeling isolated or feeling like they gave up on a career, it has allowed them to reinvent themselves.

Stacey recently enhanced these connections by attending the Moms 2.0 Summit for mom bloggers. In her estimation, everyone at the conference identifies first as a mother, but they are inspired and excited to share their passions beyond motherhood.

As a mom, attorney, and budding media mogul, Stacey is a woman who follows her dreams. She is currently writing the book, *Secrets of a Self-Styled Supermom*, where she will further reveal how she makes it all work.

Part Four

BACK TO SCHOOL—
LEGAL MOMS IN ACADEMIA

Chapter Twelve

BACK TO THE PAPER CHASE

"It has been like a dream. It is my dream job."
—Nadia Jones

AS AN ASSISTANT PROFESSOR OF PROFESSIONAL SKILLS at Florida Coastal School of Law, students often ask Nadia Jones for advice about managing the rigors of law school with their personal lives. Her own life experience in raising three children during law school and practice provides ample material for her answers. After graduating with a degree in Education from the University of Florida, Nadia chose to attend Howard University School of Law. In her first year of law school, she spent time both studying and planning her summer wedding. During her second year, she learned that she was pregnant with her first child, giving birth via caesarean section two weeks into her third year. She missed only two weeks of school, despite having a high-risk pregnancy and preterm labor. Her law school professors were aware of her situation as she prepared for leave from school.

Although Nadia's mom helped for the first few weeks and final exams, during the fall semester she and her husband did not employ a nanny or childcare; rather they maintained a delicate juggling act of responsibilities. Nadia remarks, "I think I went crazy that first semester."

She was able to choose her class schedule, and she had a lightened class load because of a previous internship. When she had class, her husband, who worked down the street, would watch the baby, or one of her girl-friends would watch her son in the student lounge.

As soon as her husband got home from work, she would go to the library to study until midnight. She was nursing at the time, so her breast pump became a constant companion. She would pump in the car or in the law school bathroom, with a book in her other arm.

By second semester they employed a nanny who alleviated some of the stress, but Nadia faced another issue—mommy guilt. After spend-ing maximum time with her son, Nadia had a hard time adjusting to another caretaker. She made good use of time while at school and got home as soon as she could. Nadia describes the time as frustrating. She felt angry at the fact that she was dealing with feelings of guilt, even though it was no one's fault. "I put a lot of pressure on myself to balance law school and family life."

Ironically, her third year of law school was her best year. She received mostly A's, which she ascribes to her complete focus and commitment to family and school. She knew she was taking time away from her family, so she made the time count. When her son was nine months old, she began studying for the bar exam. She made a detailed schedule because "not passing was not an option."

Having a child while she was in law school made Nadia much more conscious about choosing the right job after law school. She did not pursue employment with any large firms because she did not think they would support a balanced family life. While she was pregnant her sec-ond year, she was scheduled to interview with a large firm during the on-campus interview season. She cancelled the interview the day before and sometimes regrets this decision. Her mentors who were first and second year associates at large firms conveyed horror stories about unyielding pressure and enormous billable hour expectations. Their reports made Nadia realize that she needed to carve another path.

Even though she couldn't see herself being happy pursuing large-firm life, she was still somewhat jealous of classmates who were head-ing to large firms in New York or abroad. In 2002, Nadia started her first job, practicing law with a boutique law firm in Washington, DC. Her first experiences included mostly general litigation, everything from employment law to personal injury. She liked the firm and enjoyed working there but ultimately decided to make a move to Jacksonville, Florida, to be closer to her husband's family.

In Jacksonville, she chose to work at the largest firm in Northeast Florida, a big change from the small DC firm where she had been very happy. Before taking the job, she spoke with some of the associates to determine whether the work-life balance issues were addressed. She also made it clear in the interview process that she had a growing family. The firm, despite its size, was in her opinion "family friendly." However, litigation stops for no one, including small children. Nadia saw herself taking more work home and working many Saturdays during her four years in the specialty litigation department. Her first year was a big adjustment from the small firm in DC. She described this time as "a lot of coffee and a little sleep."

Neither firm had formal policies in place related to work-life balance. When Nadia became pregnant with her second child, she faced preterm issues. At that point, she went part time, generally working 8:00 A.M.–2:00 P.M. daily.

> I thought it was very difficult to be a part-time litigator because you get a fax and it is somebody filing a motion for summary judgment, or you have to prepare for a deposition. It just seemed really impossible.

She worked at the firm for four years in specialty litigation, doing commercial litigation and family law. Nadia would have liked to become a partner, but she didn't think it was possible because she wasn't able to devote the additional time involved in making partner. Not only was she expected to reach her billables, but in order to be considered for partnership, she had to participate in networking lunches, client dinners, and law firm social events. Nadia was working at her desk through lunch to try to make it home on time. She would see her male colleagues or female colleagues without children take long lunches with partners and return with great assignments. This extended to personal relationships as well with weekend excursions such as boating and golfing. Her focus had to be on just making her billable hours, which loomed over her every month. She describes it as a "miserable situation."

During this time, she would often think about what else she could do with a law degree. One particular New Year's Eve, she was working on a case until 1:30 A.M. because it was scheduled for trial the following Tuesday. Her parents were visiting and her in-laws threw a big New

Year's Eve party for the entire family. She thought to herself, "never again." Her career was not bringing her the joy that she lost by missing family events. This sentiment really hit home when she learned the following week that the trial had been continued until March.

During this time, she also felt like she was shortchanging her kids. If she wasn't able to cook, her husband would feed the kids fast food or pizza, which made Nadia feel bad about her role as a mother. Nadia's focus on family was ingrained, but she wasn't able to give 100 percent at home and at work. These thoughts were especially apparent to her as she had always known she wanted to marry and start a family at a young age. On their first date, she told her husband she wanted three kids, not necessarily knowing at the time what it would mean to her career later.

Nadia describes these years as the toughest of her career—when her oldest son was three years old and she had her newborn daughter:

> I just remember crying in the middle of the night because I was so incredibly unhappy. I was torn between, do I let my husband and nanny do it all and I just suck it up and devote my time with my family on the weekends, or do I not meet my billable hours? . . . It just seemed impossible to balance both of them.

A month after returning to work after her second pregnancy, she learned she was pregnant with her third. She felt like she had just come back from her second pregnancy because she had taken a five-month maternity leave. Her extended leave was based on factors related to her health: She experienced congestive heart failure after the second birth and was hospitalized for twelve days. She was put on complete bed rest at sixteen weeks. Her firm never gave her a hard time about her health issues or pregnancies, but she knew she was at her limit.

During her third pregnancy, she began to think about not going back to the firm. Nadia and her husband discussed her staying home for at least a year. She knew that she was not thriving in her current position. With two children and another on the way, Nadia comments, "It was either my sanity or working. I chose my sanity."

With an undergraduate degree in education, teaching was always in the back of Nadia's mind as a possible career path, but she did not think she would have the opportunity to pursue it until she was older and more experienced in the legal profession. A friend from Nadia's involvement with the Jack and Jill organization was moving and leaving her position as an assistant professor at Florida Coastal School of Law. She sought out Nadia, recommending her for the position. Nadia was ultimately hired as an Assistant Professor of Professional Skills when her third child was six months old. She assesses the transition from law firm life:

> It has been like a dream. It is my dream job. The first year was demanding only because I was learning—how to teach, the curriculum, trying getting into the groove. . . . There were many nights I was preparing for class or reading. . . . I definitely over-prepared that first year, but it wasn't as gruesome as drafting a memorandum of law or appending or preparing a hearing. Also, I can do it on my own time.

The first year, she taught three days a week. During her second year, she was able to choose her schedule. On her off days, she worked from home preparing for class. She had complete autonomy preparing for classes. She currently teaches Lawyering Process. After five years, she is now considering a transition into doctrinal classes, such as Civil Procedure.

Reflecting on her career and its various transitions, Nadia describes the hardest part of juggling motherhood with a legal career as giving up some of her own aspirations because she chose to make her family her priority:

> The hardest thing has been knowing that I am not giving my career 100 percent because of my family. It think that has been very hard for me. . . . I would have loved to have made partner, but I knew that it wasn't going to be an option with kids. The partner track—seven years of working in the coal mines to make partner—I just couldn't do it. I really believe "family first." I didn't want to miss those important times. I wanted to be able to go to school functions when I could, especially during their younger years. Now they are older, the mommy guilt has almost been cured.

At one point at the firm when she was asked to work on a big case that would require travel, she declined because of family issues. She felt a tinge of jealousy when the firm sent around a memo congratulating everyone who had worked on the case, including the associates who had the opportunity to go to trial. Nadia has some regrets at not feeling like she pursued her law career fully:

I am grateful for my job and I love my job. I think it is best at this point in my life for my family. There are times when I think, it kind of would have been nice to have been that high-powered attorney or a partner at a prestigious firm. That is what you work for in law school—to be successful and accomplished. I do feel accomplished, but maybe I took Route B instead of Route A.

Nadia is a proponent of female mentoring and acknowledges the role that mentors have played in her professional life:

It meant a lot to me. Even today, I mentor my students. I think it is really important to talk to others who have been there and who can give you advice and to talk to as many people as you can. They've done it before, so you can learn from their experiences what worked from them and what didn't work. Try to make your own path in the process.

Advice: It is all about a schedule.

In law school, one of Nadia's professors had a workshop for students who were moms on "How to be a mom and how to be successful in law school." Nadia's ears were burning during the seminar. Every word the professor said, Nadia wrote down. Her message, "It is all about a schedule," still resonates with Nadia today. She advocates strategies for working ahead. For example, on Sunday, make dinner for two days—roast a chicken and make lasagna.

Nadia is type A when it comes to her family: The well-being, comfort, and education of her children are her top priority. She has to remind herself not to extend this pressure to her children. She also has to remind herself that if things don't work out the way she planned, it is okay. Patience is important for a high-functioning mom. She is calm among chaos. Inside, she may feel like she is scrambling and losing her mind, but on the outside she is capable and confident.

I just love seeing my kids grow. Seeing them happy makes me really happy. I have nurtured my children and they are doing well.

Nadia acknowledges that two careers, along with her type-A personality can put a strain on a marriage. She and her husband have been married eleven years and have come through difficult times.

When you are a high-performing career mom, it puts a lot of strain on your marriage. I think it is difficult. One of the things I have had to learn is balancing not just managing my children, but also a happy marriage.

Nadia expects a lot from her husband. He works in commercial real estate development. They both want to do well and want a lot for their children. Initially, they employed a schedule—sharing responsibilities every other night. She expects her husband to do things as well as she would, but has had to relax her standards. She acknowledges that he has been very hands-on as a father. She sees a lot of women who don't ask their husbands for help, then become frustrated with all of the responsibility. They make time for each other by having a weekly date night.

Nadia remarks that the law can be a difficult career for a mom. Perhaps if firms embraced more alternative work arrangements, such as paired-work environments, succeeding in a law firm environment might be more attainable for working moms:

If you want to be in law practice, you have to have the right personality for it. . . . The women that do become partner and do great, most of them regret it in some way—regret that they didn't get to spend as much time with their children as other moms. It is a tough call. It depends.

In reflecting on her career as a practicing attorney and an academic, Nadia gives the following advice to women planning to pursue a career in the law while juggling a family:

- Be prepared for tough nights and tough days.
- The more support the better, whether it is a nanny or a good daycare.
- Be diligent at making the best of your time while your children are busy.
- Accept that you may not be able to go to every lunch.
- Be creative about ways to interact with colleagues at work that are not as time consuming.

Although Nadia sometimes thinks about the struggles she has faced in juggling her career, she is ultimately glad that she stayed in the legal profession and doesn't think she would have been happy as a stay-at-home mom. She wanted to achieve and do well. If she had stayed home, she feels that she would have regretted leaving her career.

In addition to her academic career, Nadia is a frequent contributor as Justice Jonsie to her blog, www.mamalaw.com. As indicated Nadia helped to establish the Blogalicious conference, now in its second year. Recently, she also started her own small practice to take on some cases. She loves academia, especially since it has given her the balanced life she needs, but she is excited to work with clients again.

With her children getting older and her position solidified at the law school, Nadia has even been able to carve out some "me" time. She recently completed her first half-marathon. As a mom, an attorney, an academic, and a blogger, Nadia is in a place where she simply works at "being happy at wherever I am in my life."

Chapter Thirteen

TRANSITIONING
TO LEGAL ACADEMIA

*"Parenting is an entirely separate job for which there
is no formal training. There is only on-the-job training.
It is significantly easier to parent while working,
when you already know how to do the parenting."*
—*Rona Kaufman Kitchen*

As the granddaughter of four Holocaust survivors, Rona Kitchen was always aware and interested in concepts related to justice, fairness, and the rule of law. In addition, her parents strongly encouraged her to pursue a legal career. Although she had an interest in becoming a teacher as well, she was happy to pursue the career in law that her parents wanted. Ultimately, she knew that her parents wanted her to have the opportunities that would go along with being a lawyer.

Hailing from Philadelphia, Rona studied Political Science at the University of Pittsburgh. During her undergraduate years, she had the opportunity to spend a Semester at Sea, which she describes as "a really fantastic study abroad experience. That really opened my eyes to things going on in the rest of the world and, if anything, only confirmed that I should go to law school." Rona's exposure to townships in South Africa dealing with the aftermath of apartheid, the effects of the genocide in

127

Cambodia, and the caste system in India, made her realize that the horrors of the Holocaust of her grandparents' generation were still very much apparent in the world.

After graduation, Rona took a year off to decide where to go to law school. During that year, she moved to Arizona in order to establish residency, choosing to go to University of Arizona in Tucson for law school. Not surprisingly, Rona loved law school and the discussion of concepts related to justice. In her words, "Definitely part of me later wanting to become a law professor was how much I really, really enjoyed and loved law school, much more than most of my friends."

During on-campus interviewing in her second year, Rona interviewed with the largest Houston law firm and got an offer. She started as an associate in the Commercial Litigation section, basically handling contract disputes between large corporations. Rona put in her time as a junior associate with the large firm. However, after two years, she realized that she felt disconnected. The firm was too big for her. She felt as if she could spend an entire day working in her office without having one conversation related to the outside world. The horrific events of September 11, 2001, happened during her time at the firm, and she began to reevaluate where she was going with her life.

A friend worked for a Houston satellite office of a Midwest-based firm. The office had a fraction (1/5) of the attorneys that the larger firm had, and Rona coveted the experience that her friend was getting. In her words, Rona's friend was "practicing law at a level where I did not feel like I was." Although there was nothing wrong with her larger firm experience, she wanted to do more than research and writing.

Upon giving notice at the firm, Rona realized that she was pregnant with her first child. Fortunately, she had a planned month off between both jobs, which coincided with the height of her morning sickness. Rona was a wreck about having to tell the new firm she was pregnant and opted to do so a few weeks after she started. She had accepted a position with the Employment Law group, and the head of her section was wonderful to her at hearing the news. She describes him as a serious lawyer who was also laid back, nice, and interested in developing young associates.

During her six months at the firm, Rona enjoyed her job tremendously. Everything her friend had said about client contact and interesting cases was absolutely true. She found the practice of employment law fascinating and recounted her happy discovery: "[I was] surprised to learn that a lot of the time I didn't feel like I was on the wrong side."

The firm policy allowed her three months of paid leave and three months of unpaid leave. Rona opted for the full six months. When it was time for her to come back, she made an appointment with the practice group leader and let him know that she was not ready. Her daughter was a difficult baby in that she would tolerate only Rona holding her. She never slept except in Rona's arms. Rona couldn't walk out of her eyesight. Having attended Bradley Natural Childbirth classes and nursing exclusively, Rona had set herself up for attachment parenting, which would not work with a full-time job. She advises other women to avoid this scenario.

The firm offered Rona the opportunity to work from home, basically performing document review on a case with which she was familiar. Her salary was prorated by the hour. She describes the work as boring, yet it allowed her the ability to be with her young daughter. The agreement was that when her daughter was fifteen months old, Rona would come back to the firm.

Ultimately, working from home was very difficult. Rona worked at night and on weekends when her husband was home. She was very sleep deprived, as her daughter still preferred to be held by Rona 100 percent of the time. The benefits of being a working mom were not there for Rona, in the sense that she was not able to escape her responsibilities at home for a few hours. She wasn't wearing nice clothes and going into an office and seeing people. For Rona, the benefits were simply being employed and getting a paycheck.

From Rona's perspective, the firm "could not possibly have been more accommodating." Leading up to the time she was scheduled to return to the firm full time, Rona was still planning to do so. However, her mind and her heart were not in the same place. Even though she planned to go back, she comments, "I never worked it out in my mind in a way that I could come to terms with." Rona had looked into quality daycare programs and had narrowed down her selection, but she hadn't signed any contracts, and deep down, she was very torn.

As an interesting contrast, the female managing partner of Rona's firm, who had two teenage children, was pregnant with her third child at the same time Rona was expecting her first. This woman had returned to work after a very reasonable amount of time and was able to handle juggling her responsibilities. In hindsight, Rona thinks one of the major differences between her and the managing partner was that the managing partner was having a third child. She clearly had a handle on parenting, while everything was new for Rona.

In Rona's case, she didn't want to go back to work full time but needed to figure out how to support her family. Wisely, she had banked a significant amount of money intentionally before she had kids, knowing that she would need a safety net. She comments:

> I knew that at some point I was going to have kids and that I was going to want to see them and be involved. I had a mom who was and still is unbelievably loving and caring and nurturing and involved. I didn't really have any plan of compromising that.

Before she was scheduled to head back to work in the office full time, Rona learned that she was pregnant again. Her daughter was fourteen months old, and the news was a happy surprise. At that point, she made the decision to leave the firm. She felt like they had been very accommodating and had given her as much as was reasonable. On her departure, the people at the firm were kind. Several people continued to send her holiday cards. She did not feel like she let them down but had mixed feelings about leaving. In her words, "I definitely felt like they were disappointed in a personal way. I think that was me. I was projecting."

Rona chose to be a stay-at-home mom until her son was fifteen months old. When their savings started to dwindle, Rona and her husband made the difficult decision for her to go back to work.

> I did not at that point want to [go back to work]. I think that if my financial situation been different, it is very possible that I would not have gone back to work at that point. I would have been happy to not go back to work. I would have been happy to stay home and I would have made my life as a stay-at-home mom. From where I am sitting now, I am so thankful that it [staying home] didn't work out for me. It was all I wanted in that moment, but I am so thankful that it wasn't an option.

After two years of being out of the legal market, Rona was fortunate to be able to go back on a part-time basis to the Family Law section of the first firm where she worked after law school. Rona took the position of a woman with three children who was leaving the firm in order to spend more time with her family. Rona's focus was to make enough money so she could be at home with the kids on some level as well. In hindsight, it was a terrific situation. Rona was considered "of counsel" and generally billed thirty hours a week, with two hours a week allotted to administrative work. If she chose to go full time, she could jump back on partnership track whenever she was ready.

Rona went into the office every day at 7:00 a.m. staying until 1:30 in the afternoon, allowing her to pick up her kids at preschool/daycare at 2:00. Despite the limited hours, Rona continued to be torn.

> As far as a schedule, it could not have been more perfect, but I really wasn't happy at the time. . . . I was still so obsessed with my kids. *Obsessed* is really the word. I was so nervous. I was a really nervous young mom. I worried about them constantly. I felt like the only way I could know they were safe and being cared for, the way they *needed* to be cared for, was if they were with me. I just did not feel good about it. Yet looking back on it, what a perfect schedule.

This situation continued for about nine months. However, during her short time at the firm, Rona suffered a miscarriage. The suddenness of the miscarriage threw her for a loop. She needed to have a DNC procedure that day, and she had limited options for people who could watch her children. Though her husband was in trial, he came home to watch the kids, leaving Rona to face the hospital and the medical procedure on her own. In this difficult situation, she started to think about how she needed to be closer to her supportive family in Philadelphia.

Very soon after that, she started looking for jobs in Philadelphia and other options. She had made peace with the fact that she financially needed to work, but she needed to find something that she was passionate about. Her husband had been a model for loving his job, and he inspired Rona. Her two goals were to move closer to family and to find a job she wanted.

Her "very loving" husband was willing to make the sacrifice and move to make Rona happy. She was so emotional about it and felt so traumatized by having been alone during her miscarriage. As a federal prosecutor, her husband began looking for positions in the Philadelphia, New Jersey, and Delaware areas.

> Advice: Becoming a law professor does not always require a law degree from Harvard or Yale.

Meanwhile, Rona had run across an interesting opportunity at Temple Law School, called the Abraham L. Friedman Fellowship that takes practicing attorneys and trains them to be law professors. She applied to the fellowship, sending a "very impassioned" essay. She was offered a position teaching Legal Research and Writing for two years, giving her some experience. Rona was also provided with wonderful mentors and guided in the process of writing a law review article.

Rona dismisses the idea that in order to become a law professor, one has to attend the most prestigious law schools, obtain the right judicial clerkship, and graduate at the top of the class. Through the fellowship route, she was able to become a doctrinal law professor. Rona shared some of the pitfalls that people encounter who do not take the fellowship route, but become Legal Research and Writing faculty.

> Once you become a Legal Research and Writing professor—not through a fellowship, a fellowship is viewed differently—but once somebody becomes a Legal Research and Writing Professor, which is oftentimes what women do, moms in particular, they pretty much are tracked as Legal Research and Writing. If you want to equate it to the law firm, it is not partnership track. It ends up being a big mistake that people make if ultimately they want to be a doctrinal law professor; if they want to be a Legal Research and Writing professor, it's fine then. Unfortunately, for reasons that I don't understand and don't agree with, Legal Research and Writing faculty are viewed as "less than" somehow in the academy.

In Rona's estimation, there are twenty to twenty-five fellowship programs at law schools across the country preparing practitioners to be law professors.

> Unless you went to Harvard or Yale, or one of those schools, or had a parent who was a law professor that could guide you through this, and did the traditional track, (The traditional track is to graduate from Harvard or Yale, clerk for a Circuit Court or the Supreme Court, work at a firm or a government agency for a year, publish an article, and become a law professor.), this [Rona's experience] is the nontraditional option, which is becoming more and more common.

Rona was unsure how much time she would be able to devote to her family as she entered legal academia. She had a sense that her hours might be reasonable as compared to partnership track at a law firm, but her motivation at the time was to secure a position that was meaningful in which she could begin to build a career, rather than just a paycheck.

> I had friends who just couldn't wait to become partner, but I was never them. I wasn't excited by it. I thought I might do it, but I was going to do it for money. There was nothing else about it that seemed tremendously appealing to me.

Advice: Finding a job that is meaningful can make all the difference.

Rona had loved law school as student—it made her feel centered and balanced in the law school environment. In hindsight, Rona could see how all of her experiences were leading her in the direction of teaching in law school. She desperately wanted to find a job that she loved, partially because she saw how happy her husband was in his job:

> It is very inspiring to see someone love their job. At the same time, when you realize you don't love your job, the obvious question is, "why don't I do something I love?"

At the same time Rona was offered the fellowship at Temple Law School, she was also offered a position in a law firm that she thought would be a great fit for her. The fellowship had a tax-free stipend of $36,000. After some thought, Rona decided to follow her heart and take the fellowship.

The fellowship was the right decision. She comments, "The fellowship was a dream and it made everything better. Finding something I loved made all the difference." Her children were older, four and two at the time, and Rona did not feel the same anxiety about being away from them. She credits her initial anxiety to being a new mom and hormonal changes from pregnancy and breast-feeding. Once she weaned her son, she felt like a new person.

In addition to enjoying the fellowship, Rona and her family moved to Montgomery County, Pennsylvania, where she grew up. The only drawback was that it required an hour commute. Rona readily shares the advice that whenever possible, it is important to live close to where you work to cut down on the commute time. In her words, "You're not at work, you are not at home. It is a total waste."

Rona worried that she wasn't able to put as much into the fellowship as her cohorts—a single woman and a dad temporarily living away from his family—because she still needed to devote time to her children. She notes the three most important things, in order of priority, when participating in a fellowship: (1) writing a law review article, (2) building connections with other law faculty, and (3) teaching legal research and writing. Rona ended up focusing on her teaching skills in Legal Research and Writing and did not spend enough time working on her law review article or connecting with faculty.

> I didn't spend any of the time doing the schmoozing and not enough time working on my article. I spent a tremendous amount of time on LRW and counseling my students and talking to them. I was really very focused on my students. I think that is just who I am. That is not something I wouldn't have not done. At the same time, I was not doing the fellowship from the strategic perspective that I should have done.

Rona became pregnant in November of the first year of the fellowship. She proposed taking a one-year break from the fellowship and was determined to make it work. Temple was fantastic about her request and allowed her the year break. Rona thought that during her year at home, she would be able to focus on her article.

> I took a year off. I thought that during that year I would really focus on my article. I would be home with my baby and focus on my article. The only reason I could have been thinking that was because I had completely forgotten what it had been like when I had been home in the past. My memory is that short when it comes to how time-consuming a brand new baby is.

Rona's year at home was wonderful, and though she worried about going back to the fellowship and leaving her one-year-old son, she was committed to making it work. Her schedule required her to teach two days a week. During the days she taught, Rona had a sitter come to the house in the event one of the kids became ill, she would still be able to teach. The other three days, her two youngest attended full-day preschool, while her daughter attended kindergarten.

As she completed her final year of the fellowship, Rona went on the job market for law faculty. She attended the Faculty Recruitment Conference held annually in Washington, DC. She and her husband decided that she was going to be serious only about jobs that would keep them in the same area. They had recently purchased a home and did not want to make another move. Rona was not confident that she would receive a job offer:

> I think my expectations were very low, and I didn't want to move. I was very happy living near family. We bought a house that I absolutely loved. My daughter was at my elementary school and I loved that. We had wonderful neighbors. Everything was quite perfect, except for the job part.

Rona describes the job market for law faculty as "extremely, extremely, extremely competitive." She had not yet published her article by the time she went to the Faculty Recruitment Conference, which in her words, "was a huge failure on my part." She was skeptical that the process would work for her, especially since they were unwilling to move. Everyone had counseled her that she would have to be completely willing to move anywhere in order for the process to be worth her time. In the back of her mind, she had decided that if she did not receive an offer she would pursue a PhD and go back into the academic market five years later.

To her credit and astonishment, Rona received an offer from Duquesne University School of Law in Pittsburgh. She had very little time to make the decision. Her husband did not want to move, and Rona was torn as well, but they ultimately decided to go for it. In her words, "Everything worked out for the best."

As a law professor, Rona is putting forth a tremendous effort to be successful. In terms of work, she feels like this is the best job she has ever had, though she works longer hours:

> I am actually working longer hours now than I ever have since having kids. It is okay. I am at a place where it is okay for me. I am okay with it. Again, I really love my job. For me, that makes all the difference in the world. I am also a more experienced mom. I am not at all the mom I was when I thought I needed to be with my kids every minute of every day. Not only do I not need it, I am very much aware of the value to them of not having me around every minute of every day.

For the last year, Rona has juggled her responsibilities with the help of a nanny, the first time she has employed childcare in her household.

Having a nanny allowed her the flexibility to shift her schedule to meet work demands in the day and evenings. She notes that in this situation she "had complete and total availability when it came to work." She also liked that she would come home to a happy and peaceful house, rather than running to pick up children at preschool or daycare, lugging backpacks and exhausted kids. When her youngest turned three and a half, Rona decided to enroll him in full-day preschool, so now all of her children are back in school/daycare settings. When they moved the family to Pittsburgh, they made the decision to use private schools. Rona feels like the school they chose is a "partner" to her in raising the children and is very supportive of them as a family.

> Advice: Academics requires long hours, but does allow for some flexibility.

Rona addresses two of the misperceptions of academia: (1) that being a law professor is flexible, and (2) that it is an easier job than climbing toward partnership in a law firm per se. She notes, "The idea that the job has flexibility is accurate. The idea that there is not a lot of work is completely false."

In terms of flexibility, Rona is very much in charge of her day. She is responsible for teaching four classes per year: Corporations (first and second semester), Labor Law, and Work Life Law Seminar. On the days that she teaches, there is no flexibility. Come what may, Rona will be in front of her class and completely prepared. She is also responsible for attending faculty and committee meetings. Other than classes and faculty responsibilities, she generally has the flexibility she needs. She prefers not to work at home because she is usually more productive in her office on campus. However, if she gets a call from the school that one of the kids is sick in the middle of the day, she is able to leave and deal with it. Rona's youngest child has been diagnosed with allergies and asthma, necessitating more doctors' appointments. Rona is able to schedule office appointments during normal business hours.

When she has an obligation that pulls her away from the office, Rona is able to make up the time on her own. She equates this type of flexibility to having your own law practice—the work needs to get done, but you can determine when and how.

Rona also dispels the rumor that academia is an easy ride. She works harder than she ever has at any job, yet laughs that her husband questions what she does all day at the office, asking if it really takes so long to prepare for classes. Rona explains,

> The only thing that has been similarly difficult to quantify or really give a fair estimation of how much time it takes is the whole thing about taking care of kids. No one knows what you're doing all day with them either. All you know is that all day you are busy. I don't know what I did all day. I didn't sit down. I didn't watch TV. I didn't talk on the phone. I didn't eat. I am not even sure if I showered. I don't know what I did do, but all I know is that I have been really busy.

In Rona's opinion, another challenge to the job is that there is always more that she could be doing. Rona wants to achieve tenured status, and realizes the time that she will need to commit. In regard to scholarship, Rona is determined to leave her mark:

> This is a job where you get to design what is going to be your area of scholarship. If you are really trying to accomplish something, you could spend an entire lifetime trying to accomplish something and spend no free time doing anything else. It is a bottomless pit the amount of time that you could spend.

Rona's area of scholarship is combining paid work with parenting. Her recent law review article, "Eradicating the Mothering Effect: Women as Workers and Mothers, Successfully and Simultaneously"[1] has been accepted to the *Wisconsin Journal of Gender, Law & Society*. She is passionate about this subject:

> I want to have an impact on what we have in place, for moms specifically, but primary caregivers all around and even all parents, to do a better job combining parenting with paid work where kids are getting what they need. I think a lot of kids don't get what they need from their parents because their parents don't have the time. It is not their fault. They don't have the time. They are not able to do what they need to do at work and also give their kids what they need. I think that is not good for our country. . . . I think it would be good for everyone if parents were able to give their kids the time they need.

In her second year as an Assistant Professor of Law at Duquesne, the work has gotten slightly easier. Rona was teaching brand new courses in her first year. She generally worked a forty-hour week, plus evenings

---

1. Rona Kaufman Kitchen, *Eradicating the Mothering Effect: Women as Workers, Successfully and Simultaneously*, 26 WISC. J. L. GENDER & SOC. 167 (2011).

and weekends. Though this might have been a miserable schedule had she been at a law firm, Rona really enjoys her work in academics:

> It is really important for me for me to feel like I know everything I need to know before I go into the classroom. I derive immense personal benefit from doing the work.

Rona also believes that being a full-time law professor with three children is meaningful to the women law students at Duquesne. Many of them are thinking of how they might combine work and family down the road. As in law firm partnership, there are not abundant examples of female law professors with young children.

In Rona's career pattern, each position and experience built on everything else. She believes that all of the decisions she made were the right decisions at the time. She comments of her pre-academic life, saying, "I don't know how much of me not being overjoyed at the firm was the firm and how much was that I was just too new as a parent to be able to enjoy that."

Teaching law is definitely Rona's calling and the career she was ultimately meant to have. In addition, her experience as a full-time working mom, a part-time working mom, and a stay-at-home mom have informed her research. Recently she gave a Continuing Legal Education Seminar on mothering and fielded a question about the subject of "mommy wars"—the idea that women who stay at home and women who work full time are in conflict. Rona answered, noting,

> I don't think there is a war between stay-at-home moms and working moms and part-time working moms. I just think that just is, first of all, a big lie. It is true that most women are all those different moms at different times in their lives. Most of us are working moms, and we are part-time working moms, and we are full-time working moms, and sometimes we are home, even if it is just on maternity leave, during our lifetimes. Really that tension is inside of ourselves, figuring out that right balance.

At this moment, Rona is happily working full time, along with her husband. But there have been times when this arrangement has not worked for her. Drawing on her experience in law and life, she is forging a career in legal academia and scholarship on paid work and parenthood.

Part Five

SETTING UP A LAW PRACTICE—HANGING OUT A SHINGLE

Chapter Fourteen

A LEGAL MOM STRIVING FOR SEAMLESSNESS

"There is nothing shameful or wrong about being pregnant or having children. . . . I think that we should celebrate that and not apologize for it."
—*Alexandra Foote*

ALEXANDRA FOOTE DESCRIBES HER ROAD to law school as a "long struggle with trying to find a way to plug in." She had a strong academic background, graduating magna cum laude from the University of Oregon in Public Policy. She was also the recipient of an award for outstanding leadership. She went on to Brown University, studying for a master's degree in Environmental Studies with a full scholarship. In graduate school, Alexandra struggled academically for the first time in her life, which made her question moving forward with the degree. She moved back to her home state of California. During this time, she met and married a lawyer. Observing his profession, she thought to herself, "This is interesting." The idea that she could use her mind, love of words and argument, and desire to effect change intrigued her. Law school also seemed like the right path because, in her words, "You go through the academic steps, and there is something for you at the end." Ultimately, she felt an assurance that she would have a job if she pursued law school, which neither her undergraduate degree in Public Policy nor her master's degree in Environmental Studies guaranteed her. She decided to go back to finish her master's degree and apply to law school.

Alexandra enrolled in University of California, Hastings College of the Law, one of the top law schools in the country, conveniently located for Alexandra in San Francisco. She loved law school. Reading cases and talking to people about the law was exactly what she wanted to do. She spent her first summer working with a dot.com established by the founder of Netscape. She spent her second summer in Stuttgart, Germany, working for a firm that was outside counsel for Daimler.

Although she enjoyed each of these experiences, she decided that she would be most satisfied championing people who were wronged. She set her sights on one of the top plaintiff's firms in the country. During her last year of law school, she positioned herself for a job with the firm by contacting attorneys at the firm about research she was doing for class on scientific evidence and disability. She offered to perform research for the firm related to the topic. She worked with a partner on her research, and the piece that she wrote was ultimately published. Alexandra initially started at the firm as a contract attorney and became an associate a few months later. Considering that the firm traditionally pulled only from the top Ivy League law schools, she was thrilled.

The work at the firm was tremendously exciting. Alexandra worked on high-profile, complicated, class action cases. The firm was known to throw associates into the fire to see if they could handle it. Some of her colleagues from top Ivy League law schools lasted only a few months. She worked long hours, sometimes 8:00 a.m. to 11:00 p.m., and weekends. It was typical for attorneys to be sleeping on their office floor, working for three solid days, or billing 370 hours in a month. The firm expected the best work product humanly possible. Alexandra gave it everything she had.

The long hours started to take a toll on her health. She had gained weight because she didn't take time to exercise, her hair was falling out, and she was getting strange rashes. She was not living her best life and felt like she was starting to deteriorate from working so hard. She also had hurt her wrist badly and found it difficult to type on the keyboard. At the end of law school, Alexandra and her husband had divorced. While at the firm, she met someone new and started to pull back from the grueling hours in order to find some balance. The partners at the firm noticed—commenting that they didn't see her on Saturdays any-more. She realized that it wasn't a place where she could sustain a career on a long-term basis.

As Alexandra's relationship progressed, she started to think about eventually having a baby and realized that it probably wouldn't work at that firm. There was little precedent for legal moms working at the firm. Alexandra didn't feel that the firm believed pregnant attorneys could pull their weight. One associate left when she got pregnant. Another woman hid her pregnancy under a poncho until her sixth month, when she made partner.

> I didn't think I could make it work. I just felt like the pace and the intensity of what I was doing was taking such a toll on my health, that I couldn't even pull back to take care of my wrist. How in the world would I care for another human being? That is the sort of deal that you make there—it was 100 miles per hour every day.

After four years, she left for a midsized defense firm. Alexandra was very conscious of what type of firm she wanted—more laid back, family friendly, with a manageable billable hour requirement.

At the new firm, almost all of the partners had families. Alexandra was encouraged by the fact that the female partners seemed to find a way to make it all work. The firm had a friendly vibe where attorneys were proud of their community activities and their family lives. She was also attracted to the type of clients that the firm had—midsized compa-nies and small businesses. Alexandra felt like she could be a rainmaker, as she had always enjoyed making connections with people and being a resource.

Shortly after she started with the firm, Alexandra got married. The firm gave her time off for her wedding and honeymoon. Two years later, in 2008, she had her first child. She admits that her pregnancy was a dif-ficult time for her career:

> I had a really difficult pregnancy. That was hard for me. I felt like the partners I worked with really appreciated my work. People certainly seemed to appreciate my rainmaking potential and the fact that I started bringing in business really early on as an associate. Pregnancy made it really, really hard. I was anemic and I couldn't shake the ane-mia. I had never had my body let me down like that. I was sick and I felt terrible. I just couldn't do as much work as I wanted to do even

though I would push myself so hard. I don't know if people would say around me, "That anemic, pregnant lady, she is really not doing her job." I think people were probably sympathetic, but for me it was devastating to not feel like I could just power through like I usually did.

Due to premature labor pains, Alexandra went on maternity leave slightly early but was able to carry the baby full term. She was given three months paid maternity leave and ultimately took eight months off, primarily because of the economic turn of 2008. While she was on maternity leave, the economy crashed. She was at home caring for her newborn, listening to news about law firm layoffs. As her time to return to work approached, she learned that one of her colleagues who had recently had twins was laid off. Alexandra was concerned that if she went back to the firm, there would not be enough work for her, so she volunteered to take a few more months off unpaid.

After eight months, she determined that she couldn't afford not to work anymore and came back to the firm. She immediately noticed that a pall had settled over the firm and the legal profession. There was less work, and people were afraid of losing their jobs. Partners needed to make their billable hour commitments, so there simply was not enough work to go around. Though she returned full time, like many other associates Alexandra was starved for work, so she proactively volunteered to go to part time.

Fortunately for Alexandra, she was able to land a huge case on her own. She was working so many hours on the case that she was able to return to full-time hours. However, the firm did not reinstate her full-time salary because they wanted to wait until the hours averaged out between the part-time hours she had been working and her new full-time hours. This did not sit well with her:

> That kind of bothered me because when you are working full time, especially when you have a little one at home, you really feel the sacrifices that you are making. . . . I was a little put off by "We need to have your average hours work out." . . . There wasn't the work there for me. It wasn't like it was my fault. I kind of chafed under that. I didn't like that. I kept at it for a while. I was also still attracting a lot of business. I would see my numbers every month, see that I was bringing in enough money that I was almost free for the firm. I was bringing in more money than my salary. So I wondered why they wouldn't bring me up to full time. I didn't want to be a pest about it.

So I just thought maybe when I am up for partner—maybe that is when this all will work out.

Then Alexandra got pregnant again, unexpectedly. She didn't feel the firm was as receptive to her news this time around. In her words, "I did feel like getting pregnant the second time knocked me out of the game." No one ever said anything specifically to her, but she had a strong feeling that her value within the firm had been downgraded.

> I felt like when I was pregnant again, something had changed. Whereas people who were patient with me with the first one, this one I didn't feel that way. No one ever said anything to me. There wasn't anything specific about it, but I just had a feeling. Then partnership was announced. There were people who were elevated as partner who were behind me, who had been there less time.

Alexandra had focused her time and attention on building business and rainmaking. The theme of bringing in clients was strongly emphasized at firm retreats and by the partners. She felt as if she was getting a mixed message. Essentially the firm wanted her to bring in business but also wanted her to bill tons of hours and get trial experience in order to make partner. Alexandra understands it from a business perspective, but practically because she spent time cultivating contacts, she couldn't bill as heavily. She focused on her strength of connecting people and building a book of business as a strategy, but the firm couldn't look past the fact that she had worked part time. They wanted her to bring her average up, so that she compensated for when she was part time. She simply could not catch up under that model. Ironically, she was making her billable hours, but it didn't matter.

> I was finally making my hours, but it didn't matter. That was the ultimate frustrating thing. I was trying to do everything and then feeling like I wasn't being a very good mom. I was coming home pretty late. . . . I didn't feel like I could make it all work.

In addition to these professional developments, after having her second child in 2010, Alexandra felt like her "superstar status" at the firm had fallen. She started to think critically about the future of her career and the possibility of going out on her own. She had a book of business and a really big case on the horizon.

Alexandra had the opportunity to partner with a more seasoned lawyer who came out of partial retirement to work with her. He had experience building a firm and could help her navigate the big case she landed. They made an agreement and formed an Oakland-based firm, Farber & Foote, which has been going strong for a year.

Her partner is a single guy without children. They work very well together, but Alexandra has had to educate him about the challenges of being a working mom. She can't talk about a case on the phone when she is in the middle of dinner or giving the kids a bath. With her new arrangement she is able to bring her infant daughter to the office without judgment. She is able to work her schedule to fit her life. She reflects:

> When I travel for my cases to take depositions and such, I can do whatever it is that I need to do to get the support that I need in terms of who I bring and how I do it. I don't have to worry about what the firm thinks of me or anything like that. It is just me now. It is incredibly freeing.

Advice: Starting a firm gives you the freedom to set your own rules.

Alexandra has chosen to incorporate her children into her work as much as possible. She does not try to hide her dual role as an attorney and a mother. As she comments, she is comfortable showing up for a deposition with her kids in tow checking into a hotel room. The kids might be with her in the hotel restaurant at breakfast along with their nanny or au pair. When setting up the deposition schedule for the day, she is okay asking the question, "Can you tell me exactly what time we will break at lunch because I need to breastfeed my baby?" She has never had pushback, and all of the lawyers she has worked with have accommodated her. In her words, "This is what my reality is, and I am doing my job."

After several years of litigating in other firms, Alexandra was also happy to come to the realization that she is a named partner in her own firm and has earned her place at the table among the larger-firm attorneys. In her words, "They can think whatever they want of me or my case, but I am still there; I am at the table."

Having a full-time law practice does require juggling on the home front. From the time she had her oldest child, Alexandra has employed full-time nannies; however, she recently became involved with an au pair program. This gives her the childcare hours and flexibility she needs.

The au pair lives with their family, giving them a certain number of hours per week, and has committed to one-to-two years with the family. Thus far, Alexandra has enjoyed the experience. However, unlike professional nannies, taking on a younger woman from a foreign country does create another semi-mothering relationship. A level of confidence and experience came with the position of nannies. With an au pair, Alexandra feels responsible for her and needs to make sure that she is making the right judgments with the kids. It is a little more stressful because she is checking in more often to make sure that the kids are okay and that the au pair is okay. She also learned that according to regulation au pairs are not to be left alone with children under the age of three months.

Having full-time care to help her manage the children is especially important in Alexandra's case, because her husband also has a demanding career as a world-renowned chef. His San Francisco restaurant, Coi, is two-star Michelin rated and has been recognized as one of the 50 best restaurants in the world. He writes for *Food and Wine*, along with the *New York Times* and other publications, and has a cookbook in publication. Alexandra was well aware of the demands of his career when they married and decided to have children. She loves what he brings into their lives, especially his commitment to the sustainable food movement.

Although she knew his time with their children would be limited by his work, Alexandra jokes that the book *Getting to 50/50: How Working Couples Can Have It All by Sharing It All,* by Sharon Meers and Joanna Strober, sometimes is placed conspicuously on the coffee table or conveniently left on her husband's pillow. However, she is grateful that when her husband begins to see the panic in her eyes as she tries to manage everything, he is happy to take the kids for a few hours while she finishes up a brief. They are both handling so much in terms of career and home life, that sometimes it just comes down to who cries "uncle" first.

Alexandra feels that it is important for her children to see her work, as well as her husband. In her words, "Working is an integral part of being a member of society." When she was at home for eight months on maternity leave, she was certainly still working—cooking, cleaning, gardening, and so forth. Now that she is primarily practicing law as her work, her children can witness it when they come to her office. There is always work to be done, whether in the home or professional spheres. Giving her children this sense of a work ethic is important to her.

> I like to think that it sets an example for my children that women work just as much as men work. There is not this disconnect.

When her husband takes the kids to farmers markets and cooks test recipes in their kitchen, he is able to incorporate them into his career. Noting the differences between men and women, Alexandra comments,

> I don't see my husband wondering if he should still be working as a chef. I see him wanting to be able to be present more but not thinking he somehow shouldn't be doing what he is doing. And so I don't think I should be questioning being a lawyer, because that is my career and my professional role. For me, the challenge is how can I bring my children more into [my career] so there is not that disconnect.

Despite her commitment to her career, Alexandra does sometimes wonder whether she is shortchanging her kids. Although this gives her pause, she also thinks that she has bright, delightful children that don't need her as much as she might think they do. They are simply enjoying their life and surroundings. Overall, she doesn't need to create experiences for them—they are doing fine "just being." This doesn't lessen her internal struggle:

> The hardest thing is feeling inside myself that I am not doing either one as well as I would like to be. I am pulled flat-out to the end of my limits every day. I always wish there was more I could do—either on my cases or for my kids. Sadly, it is the cases that often get the extra gild because we need to do that as professionals, so I will do that extra bit there, but I feel like it takes the extra bit away from being a mom. I don't get to be the mom at the preschool who volunteers and does all the cool stuff that some of those moms do who don't have jobs. They are really involved. They seem to have a life where they are more involved, and for me, I can't even open my e-mails from the school. I don't have time. In that sense, I feel like I am not the shiny mom I want to be.

Alexandra also notes that sometimes after a particularly intense day, she feels depleted and has trouble plugging into the kids. Of course, she still makes dinner, bathes them, and puts them to bed, but she notices that she might not take the time to snuggle on the couch. In her words,

I am not the mom of my dreams. I am more of a scaled-back version of that. I don't know if that essentially will ever matter for my children. I don't know if they'll notice or miss it or if it matters, but it is just that I hold myself to some grotesquely abnormal standard of what I think mothers should be and what lawyers should be.

From her own upbringing, Alexandra had a strong example of a working mom. Her mother returned to school as an adult and became an archeologist. She incorporated her kids into her work and found a way to integrate her work into her role as a mother. Alexandra never had a sense of the separation between her mother's work and home life. If her mom was at work, they would go to her office, where Alexandra worked part-time as a teenager. Her vision of the world was that her kids were welcome to be part of her work life, therefore creating seamlessness between personal and professional spheres.

In Alexandra's opinion, the law is not a good career for a mom. The legal profession has always been modeled on a typical 50-year-old, male, white lawyer, and that model needs to change. She comments,

> I really want it to be. It is not now, but I think it should be. . . . It needs to be okay for a lawyer to have a family and to have that family life be acknowledged. There is something weird about the practice of law where you are almost like this robot lawyer that doesn't do anything except lawyer. You kind of have to present this hyper-professional front of being nothing but the advocate you set out to be. To admit that you have a life, or have other things going on, softens you somehow.

Perhaps some of this outlook can be attributed to her experience as a litigator. Litigation is an adversary practice, with the lawyers sometimes akin to warriors. The mentality is, "I will crush you, I will give you more discovery that you can ever handle." This "take no prisoners" attitude doesn't jibe with the prevailing image of being a mother, taking care of small children, and breastfeeding.

In Alexandra's opinion, if more mothers practiced law, the profession would have to adopt different expectations. Women should not have to choose whether to be an attorney or a mother, but can find a way to maintain a work life and a home life that may not need to be mutually exclusive. She notes, "The more women there are in the profession, the more normal that might be."

As it is, Alexandra sees too many women leaving the profession—giving up good jobs with firms because they just can't make it work after having a baby. She also has seen new mothers that get laid off, thereby creating an inadvertent housewife. Part of the difficulty in managing a legal career as a mom comes down to having only a certain amount of childcare:

> The most stressful thing about being a mom and being a lawyer is that you have your childcare for a certain amount of time. You know you are covered. You can spend those hours doing the work. When stuff comes outside of that time, you've got a real problem. You just can't not feed your kids or hold them or whatever it is you need to be doing at the time. If there is no one else to do it, it is you. You can't do that and draft a brief at the same time. It is impossible.

In her experience working for other people in litigation, they may not be sensitive to the fact that a legal mom has childcare available only from 9:00 a.m. to 6:00 p.m. Saying, "I can't get this project done in the timeframe needed," doesn't make a legal mom a go-to person within the firm. From Alexandra's perspective, "The worst thing is that there is nothing you can do about that."

Advice: Establish control over your work schedule as much as possible.

In her practice it is very important that things are measured and that she has a certain amount of control. She needs to be responsive to her clients and finds that in litigation, she can look ahead and make a plan based on a discovery or trial schedule. She comments, "I find that I have more of that now than I did before, but there are still those wild cards out there."

Alexandra is proud of the boutique practice that she is building. She believes in her clients and knows she is doing important work to help effectuate their goals. She hopes that her practice will eventually be steady enough that she has more balance and can get a little more sleep. Like many working moms, she doesn't take time for herself—manicures, regular haircuts, and an exercise schedule may be a thing of the past, for now. However, she is happy and inspired by the work she is doing in environmental litigation.

Recently, Alexandra was working on a large-scale wildfire case. She found a sense of camaraderie with two other legal moms working for the government on the case. She wasn't the only attorney in the room dealing with childcare issues and making sacrifices. In a way, they all have a common background from which they were operating.

Alexandra considers herself part of a group of women lawyers "who have their claws in and are not leaving." Colleagues at big firms who might be struggling but are making it work inspire her. By sheer numbers and not making excuses for the experience of motherhood, Alexandra truly believes legal moms can change the profession. She gives the following advice:

> Do it. Go forth and practice law. Have your family. Make your claim on the profession because it is open to us now. Now, our trick is to shape the profession to fit it to accommodate us. That is really the next step. It is not going to happen if women drop out of it and if women concede to the difficulty of managing a practice and managing a family. Let's make the practice accommodate us. Make it normal to make mothers of children to be in the practice and for the practice to accommodate that.

The question of how to manage as a working mother isn't necessarily confined to the legal profession. In Alexandra's opinion, it just needs to be okay to be a working mother in general. Perhaps by creating a home life and career that are more seamless, legal moms can find a solid footing.

> Our society still seems to have this notion that if you have children you need to be at home with them. It is either home life or work life, and the two don't mix.

By mixing the career and family through starting her own practice, Alexandra hopes to find the right balance.

Chapter Fifteen

THE "WICKED-AWESOME" LEGAL STEPMOTHER

"I have the girls, and I feel like I have such a big part
of their lives. . . . I may not be their biological parent,
but I have raised two children and it is no different. . . .
There probably is some difference, but I will
never know what it is."
—*Jill Krolikowski*

JILL KROLIKOWSKI IS A WOMAN who is not to be deterred when she is on a mission. Graduating from a small high school, she was one of three or four girls to go on to college. Her high school guidance counselor asked her why she wasn't headed to community college. Jill chose to enroll in Michigan State University to study Political Theory and Constitutional Democracy at James Madison College. During her time at Michigan State, she worked at the Council against Domestic Assault as a legal advocate and in a law firm as an intern. She applied to one law school, Wayne State University in Detroit. She was not initially accepted; however, this did not defeat her passion for the law.

She took a job as a legal secretary in a small insurance defense law firm, and at the urging of one of the firm attorneys, she reapplied to law school. This time she was accepted at Wayne State University Law School. Jill worked as a paralegal during the day and attended Wayne State as a night student, graduating with honors from the law school that had initially rejected her.

Jill loved her job as a paralegal. She was given a lot of responsibility, including travelling with attorneys and assisting in trial. Despite liking the firm, she knew she did not want to work there as an attorney because she felt the other attorneys would always view her as a paralegal. She chose to interview with a larger firm in Troy, Michigan, during on-campus interviews. She was given an offer as they were impressed with her contacts and experience.

After working as an attorney for two years at the firm in Troy, a large Michigan law firm gave Jill an offer that would double what was her then current salary. She loved the firm in Troy, but the salary hike was too good to pass up.

After three years practicing insurance law, Jill felt personally dissatisfied with her position. She felt a need to be more herself and take 100 percent control of her life, including what to wear, with whom to have lunch, and how to spend her nonbillable time. She quit her job and went on a three-week yoga retreat in Ojai, California. While there, she made the decision to take out her savings and start her own firm:

> I knew that there were many ways for people to be successful, and I didn't have to fit into the mold that a firm prescribed to me to be successful.

Jill knew she could do a good job with clients, and despite having only five years of experience as an attorney, she was ready to take the leap and start her own firm. She describes her decision as a "light bulb moment" when she finally realized that she was the only one who truly had an interest in the development of her career, not the firm and not the attorneys for whom she worked:

> I am not working for people I don't believe in. I believe in myself. When a person is ready to start their own firm, they look at their bosses and realize that those people have no interest in the success

of their career. They have none. Only you have interest in the success of your career.

She was prepared to give it her all, which fit into her grand plan as she had no plans to ever have children. She could focus her time completely on her career and enjoy its rewards.

Jill became romantically interested in an attorney at another firm before she went out on her own. Things fizzled, but when she set up her own practice, he sent her an e-mail joke and they reconnected. He became a resource for her on family law matters, and they rekindled their earlier romance. They began dating in February of 2008. Jill knew that he had two young daughters that lived with him full time. She met the girls in May after they both knew that they had serious feelings that would likely lead to marriage.

Jill jokes that they got married to spend time together, because they were both incredibly protective of the girls, aged six and seven at the time, and wanted to preserve values within the household. Jill would come to the house for dinner, but would always leave afterward. After much consultation, they decided to elope on their own without the girls in October of 2008. The girls knew that they were getting married over the weekend, but Jill and her new husband wanted to be sensitive to their feelings, knowing that children may see a parent's second marriage as the end of a hope of their own parents ever getting back together. They wed at the Toledo Ohio Circuit Court, which granted same-day wedding licenses, and had lunch at Arby's afterward.

For someone who had no plans ever to have children, Jill describes the transition moving into the house as "very difficult": "I didn't have nine months of preparing and planning, but I knew what was right for the kids."

Her husband had raised the girls from the ages of three and one on his own as a single dad, and their home needed a woman's touch. Jill fell into the role of mother quickly. She instinctively knew the girls needed her to fill a void. She could weigh in on hair and clothes in a way that their father wasn't able to do. Jill rejected the idea of being a "detached stepparent" because it was not an option for her situation. The girls were very young and needed her to step up. As a grown-up, Jill simply refused to ignore the pressing needs of two small children who hadn't had a say in their own parents' divorce. Despite not being a biological relative to the girls, Jill marvels at her role as their stepmother:

> You have a chance to influence children's lives. . . . They talk like me, they dress like me. It is really interesting to see how you have an influence on another person. I am just their stepmother. I am not a biological relative to them.

The girls have completely accepted Jill. They like her and she likes them, but she does acknowledge challenges with being labeled as a stepparent. She has all of the responsibility of raising the girls, without any of the authority, which can be difficult when dealing with other parents or schools.

> I pay for the kids. I am there at 3:30 when they get out of school. I worry about them. I care about them. I arrange childcare when I have a deposition, or a court meeting, or something I can't get home for. I make sure that they have matching socks every day and that their clothes are clean and folded and that their rooms are nice and they have nice things. I am expected to do all of those things. Women expect me to provide for them . . . but when I do, they say, "You are just their stepmother." When I go to pick them up from school or get involved in a school function, the other mothers have a real hard time with me. I'm just a stepmother. They want me to pay for everything. They want me to send in the checks for the school for the school party . . . They don't want me to have the authority of saying what is going to happen with the girls.

Society generally doesn't understand her position as a custodial stepparent. Though the girls live with her and she needs authority in order to provide the care that they need, she does not have it. Ironically, she also gets some backlash from other people, even clients, who don't understand why she is putting so much into raising two girls who are not hers biologically:

> People don't understand why I am doing it. Everyone says, "They are your stepdaughters, it is not your job."

As a stepparent, Jill has no legal rights in regard to the children. Everything that she has done for the girls makes no difference in a court system or the school system. She is able to pay the doctor's bills, but technically she is not able to take her stepdaughters to the doctor unless she has a release signed by her husband. In Jill's opinion, the law needs to evolve to allow a committed, healthy stepparent to have some authority in the best interests of the children.

Yet, despite these challenges, Jill made the girls' care her top priority. Her husband needed to provide financial support for them, and someone had to fill the role of caring for them. The girls had been in full-time childcare or after-school care their entire lives. Shortly after they married, Jill had an unfortunate incident with the after-school childcare provider.

She had gotten into the habit of trying to end her days as early as possible so she could be there to pick the girls up from aftercare. One particular day, she told the girls that she would pick them up around 4:00. The aftercare program allowed her to pick them up anytime between 3:30 and 6:00. Because of a traffic issue, she didn't make it to the school until 4:30. The girls were hysterical, thinking she had forgotten them. The care provider berated her. Jill was upset—this program was supposed to help her manage the kids after school, and instead of dealing with the girls' fears, they had escalated the situation. After leaving, she told the girls that they were never going back, and from that day on, she would always be home by 3:30 for them.

After a short time, Jill discovered how difficult this promise was, and she made the decision to set up her practice at home:

> I moved my entire firm to my house. I moved my copiers there, all of my desks, all of my computers, my employees—they would work on the dining room table. I would work in my office in the house. That way, I was home. That also helped in the summer. I did not want them in daycare for the summer. I did not want them going to Montessori. So I just worked at home, and they stayed at home for the summer for the first time ever in their lives. . . . It was wonderful for them. It made them better kids. I knew that if I stayed home with them, they would like me for doing that for them. And we would get along better. That was important. I wanted all of us to get along. I was definitely willing to make that sacrifice. I knew it would help them when they got older. I want them to be good kids.

Her practice had been established for two years before she moved it home; nevertheless, she noticed a dip in her bottom line after making the transition. It was difficult to keep up the intensity of her practice while working in her house. She eventually made the decision to rent an office again close to home, but continues to be home at 3:30 or relies on her support system as backup.

In the two and a half years since she married, Jill has been able to work it all out with the help of her husband and her mother. She doesn't like hiring babysitters and would prefer to have family involved with the girls. When she can't make it home by 3:30, her mom fills in or her husband comes home early.

Shutting down her workday by 3:00 can sometimes pose a problem for her busy litigation practice. She recalls one situation where she realized that a meeting with her client and a probation officer was running late and that she needed to call her husband to meet the girls at home. She told the probation officer that she needed to take a quick break to make a phone call to secure childcare. The probation officer was angry and threatened that if she left the meeting, it was over and her client would remain in jail for another month. Jill was incredulous and simply wouldn't accept it. She responded, "I am not going to come back in four weeks and do another meeting with you and have my client languish in jail for four weeks because I need to make a phone call to get child-care." In Jill's opinion, the law just doesn't make it easy for mothers to be lawyers.

Jill also notes how judges schedule their dockets to begin at 8:00 a.m., before her stepdaughters' school day starts. She feels that she is between a rock and a hard place. She needs to get the girls off to school, but if she doesn't attend court, she is held in contempt and belittled and berated in front of her colleagues. Jill is respectful of the judiciary but expresses frustration when she shows up for a 9:00 hearing that doesn't begin until 11:30, noting that it becomes problematic when she has an obligation with the kids. But she acknowledges that saying that you have children and using their needs as an excuse is akin to blaming your secretary for errors:

> If you say, "I have children. I have to worry about childcare today," . . . I just don't feel it is acceptable to even say that.

In Jill's opinion, such excuses wouldn't matter anyway. Therefore, she makes sure that she can reach her husband, her mother, or her brother by cell phone or text message to take care of the girls if she gets stuck. Generally, she sees her own situation as fortunate. She is able to set her own time for depositions because she is completely in charge of her schedule. As a litigator, Jill has to deal with court timelines, but she works it out. She is particularly grateful that her mother is retired and can help out with the kids, despite living an hour away.

> Advice: Build a support system. It cannot be done on your own.

Jill doesn't see the legal profession changing to be more supportive to legal moms, but notes that women find a way to work it out:

> Staying at home with your kids, or having a part-time schedule, or just having a flexible schedule is only for a short period of time in your whole career. It is four or five-to-ten years, and our careers are spanning forty. If firms would be more flexible about that, they would have the loyalty of women who would stay then for another 20 or 30 years.

Now that she is in her thirties, she sees a lot of her attorney friends having babies and notes that they are employing support through full-time nannies or having family members (retired parents, for example) take care of the kids. Some of them have taken jobs that allow for greater flexibility than the typical large law firm jobs. Jill has seen many women dial down to a part-time law firm schedule after having children. She notes that with her current schedule she can work as much as she wants, or as much as she needs to, and is making twice what a part-time firm attorney would make, yet Jill has the flexibility to be the legal mom she wants to be:

> It is very, very flexible. I can do whatever I want. I set my own schedules. I take my own clients. There is no one telling me what to do. There is no one telling me I need to go to an evening function or I shouldn't be going. The thing is I have been very successful. It has worked out. I am making a nice amount of money. . . . Basically, I am very happy.

Jill has been offered positions over the last few years but has turned them down to preserve the flexibility that she has to take care of the girls' needs. Though her income is erratic, as she is primarily practicing personal injury law, Jill is happy with the overall amount of money that she makes. She favors the flexibility over the stability of a "normal" job.

She also loves to see the impact that her career has on her girls. Jill thinks it is wonderful for them to see her work and earn money for the family. When she settles large cases, she will explain the implication to them and include them in the way that she chooses to spend the money. After a lucrative case, she and the girls redecorated their rooms to celebrate.

She does acknowledge the sacrifices she has made in taking on a family. Financially, Jill's personal spending has taken on a new theme. She used to wear $1,000 Gucci suits and travel to New York, buying multiple pairs of Manolo Blahniks in cash. She would never do this now, and most of her current wardrobe has come from Target. She also had an active social life, eating in every expensive restaurant. At this point, she hasn't had a designer meal in over a year. Instead, she uses any disposable income to pay for braces or summer camp. In regard to her former financial life, she comments, "I miss that, but it is okay." In Jill's opinion, deferring her own wishes for the sake of the girls is what makes a good parent.

Jill also loves her work and has had to sacrifice time to childrearing. Because she is self-employed, the more she works, the more she gets paid. This can be a frustrating dilemma, but she is certain that she is making the right decisions because in ten years, the girls will be launched off to college and the time she spends now is what will count.

Jill truly enjoys parenting the girls. She was particularly tickled when one of the girls wore a suit to picture day and attempted to resolve a dispute among friends using a legal pad to write down questions that might help them see eye-to-eye. One of the reasons Jill became an attorney was to influence people, and she finds satisfaction influencing and directing the girls in positive ways.

Advice: When starting a firm, find mentors and support from the legal community

---

Jill currently mentors a group of women interested in starting their own firms. She credits the initial support she had from attorneys as a key reason why her practice has been so successful. Not only did lawyers give her work, they also offered her loans and counsel on tricky cases. In her words, "I have asked for help . . . with the kids . . . with my practice . . . I have asked for help." As she is now in her ninth year of practice, she has the following advice for others on how to make it work:

- Keep overhead low.
- Choose clients carefully.
- Choose clients you like. You will be more apt to do a great job and be more interested in the case. (For example, Jill will not take on contentious divorce cases.)
- Call every attorney you know to tell them about your new practice. (Jill has never advertised and obtains all of her clients through referrals from other attorneys and satisfied clients. Jill was an active member of several bar associations as a single woman when she had the time to devote to them.) Use these contacts.
- Trust yourself.

Jill notes that she has taken on two male partners who also wanted greater work-life balance and time with their children. The issues of raising children are not exclusive to women. Jill has found that discussing the kids has provided a very positive bonding experience with other lawyers. It is gratifying for her to hear people say what a difference she is making in the girls' lives.

Having now been a stepmother for two and a half years, Jill sees the girls as her first priority, with her job, husband, and self lower on the list. But she knows that when the girls are older, there will be time to devote to her career and marriage in a more focused way. Despite the sacrifices she has made, Jill remarks, "I don't have a maternal instinct. I never have. I never thought I would get married. I never thought I would have children."

Her path has taken a different turn than her original course, but with the girls now nine and ten years old, Jill is proud of where she is in her life and her role as a stepparent. As a legal mom, she hopes her influence will carry through as the girls choose their own path:

What I've shown them is that women can work. . . . We should be able to take care of ourselves whether we need to or not.

Chapter Sixteen

THE "SKY'S THE LIMIT" SINGLE MOM

*"I don't think my career has affected my motherhood,
and I don't think my motherhood has affected my career
in any negative, detrimental way. Instead, they enhanced
each other. . . . You can definitely do it and be happy."*
—Vy Nguyen

VY NGUYEN ALWAYS HAD A DESIRE to help people and set her sights on being a doctor or a lawyer from a young age. A few lab classes that required her to cut into specimens while she was at the University of Houston as an undergraduate convinced her to pursue a degree in Political Science and apply to law school, rather than pursue a career in medicine.

As a college senior, Vy learned that she was pregnant. Although the news was unexpected, she describes it as a blessing. She was working at a health insurance company and attending school full time, and some of the people around her discouraged her from continuing with the pregnancy. They told her to be realistic. She had only one year left at the University of Houston and plans to go on to law school. In their opinions, it made more sense for her to have an abortion and to think about being a mother after she was done with law school. Vy was not swayed by their arguments and knew she could do it. In her mind, she had no choice. She was absolutely going through with the pregnancy, despite the fact that her relationship with the father had fizzled. She was prepared to be a single mother.

Vy's mom and family were an incredible support to her during this time. She had her son, Mikey, in December of her senior year, four days after her calculus final. He arrived two weeks early. She finished her final semester and took a year off from school. She applied to Thurgood Marshall Law School in Houston and started in fall 2003.

Vy loved law school. Even now as she walks into the school, she feels revitalized and liberated. She describes her first year as tough but worth it, and she emphasizes her "great classmates." The law school was very welcoming to her as a mother. Although she never asked for any accommodations, the school made it clear to her that support was there if she needed it. As a mom, she did not feel isolated and was pleasantly surprised to meet so many other parents in her classes, even a mom with five children. From her perspective, being a mom was not an issue for her because no one could tell parents from nonparents—they were all too busy working hard studying the law:

> I never felt isolated. I was fearful that I would be an outcast or by myself, or a loner, but I was not in any way.

Vy advises women considering having a child in law school that it absolutely can be done. In her words, "If anything, it only makes you work harder as a mom." Some of her law school classmates became pregnant during law school, and it was a cause for celebration. They threw baby showers and enjoyed the excitement of new life. However, Vy cautions that law school is a different world, far more demanding than college. She was careful to set a certain number of hours to read and brief. She also recorded on the calendar what weeks would be more demanding—when she would need additional childcare. She also tried to keep a good schedule with Mikey as much as possible.

On a side note, Vy and Mikey's father reconciled and married during her first year in law school; however, they separated three years later around the time she got her bar results. Vy became a single mom as she began practicing law.

Vy hounded a prominent female Vietnamese attorney for her first job after law school. She wanted to work under a smart, seasoned lawyer from whom she could learn. She was thrilled to get the job at the small civil litigation firm as an associate. As an extra bonus, the firm was only ten minutes from home.

Originally, she was assigned family law cases, one of the practice areas in which Vy did not want to work, but her mentor wanted her to get family law experience. Vy ended up loving family law practice. Ironically, working in family law helped her have perspective in her own life. Seeing the drama of what her clients went through reinforced the idea that she knew she never wanted her son to go through such difficulties. She worked to shield him from the problems of divorced parents. Despite the fact that she is no longer with Mikey's father, they still see each other and support Mikey at events and holidays.

Vy describes her early years as an attorney as challenging, especially juggling her role as a single mom and a novice lawyer:

> Starting off a new path being a new lawyer and all the rigors and demands of that, and being a good mom, being a single mom, and not letting any of the emotional effect manifest or show while being his mom was one of the hardest things. [I was] balancing everything and being a healthy mom for him.

Advice: Carve out time for family life.

Vy was also fortunate to have tremendous support from her family and from her ex-husband's family. Her mother cared for Mikey as an infant and toddler when Vy was in school or working. When she studied for the bar exam, everyone helped out—Mikey's father, Vy's siblings, and both sets of grandparents. As he went to preschool, her mom or Mikey's dad would pick him up. Vy relates that she always had Plan A, Plan B, and Plan C, so that there would never be any question about Mikey's care. Even now, after school, Mikey goes to her mom's house or home with his father.

Vy has always worked to maximize her time with her son. Some of her successful strategies have been working from home whenever possible, finishing up her work at the office, leaving work at the office, and not working on the weekends, when she tries to reserve time to do fun things with Mikey.

> There were times when I was worried whether I could really make it happen, and on top of it, making sure that he was doing well in school.

After a year, Vy felt ready to fly from the nest of her mentor's law firm and strike out on her own. She resigned, and some of her clients followed her as she set up her own practice. After only three months on her own, she got an offer she could not refuse from a corporate client. She was asked to come on as general counsel for the company. The job came with a good, steady salary and terrific benefits. Although she was torn, Vy ultimately decided to take the corporate counsel position and give up her dream of having her own firm.

Working in-house, Vy was at the mercy of the corporation as her sole client. She had a very demanding boss with whom she clashed about the limits of her dedication to the company. On a particular occasion, she was in Washington, DC for work and scheduled to fly back early in the morning to make it home on time for her son's musical show at school. Vy credits the fact that she never misses Mikey's important events with one of the reasons why he is such a happy and well-adjusted kid. Her boss told her she had to stay in Washington longer to resolve a particular issue. Essentially, he gave her an ultimatum—if she didn't stay in Washington, she might lose her job. Vy explained that she had already told her son that she would make it to his musical show, and she was not going to go back on her promise to him. Vy chose to leave Washington, DC, to attend her son's event knowing that she might not have a job when she returned to Texas. She also realized that most people would not agree with her decision—jeopardizing a coveted job for a family obligation. However, this situation and others demonstrated to her boss that Vy was serious about her role as a mother. She was confident in her decision:

> Because I am a lawyer, if I don't work for you, don't worry, I know I can work for someone else. That was probably one of the most stressful experiences I had during my career.

During her time as corporate counsel, Vy always felt there was a struggle in balancing work and family and whether she was going to concede to the corporate pressure. Having gone through a divorce, Vy felt like she had to be there for her son. She simply couldn't be a workaholic and the mother she wanted to be.

Vy worked for the company for two years until another company acquired them. As they reevaluated whether they needed a general counsel, Vy felt it was good time for her to transition back to her dream of having her own firm. However, this time around, she chose not to go it alone but to take on a partner. For Vy, having her own firm has been a whirlwind for the last year, but she loves every minute.

> **Advice: Be selective about the cases you take on.**

Balancing work and family are much more manageable for Vy now with her own firm because she has an office in her house. Yet she still struggles with being present with her son at times. She comments that when she is involved in a heavy litigation case, her mind might be on pleadings and discovery when her son is trying to talk to her. Vy can be hard on herself when she is not able to pay attention to her son entirely:

> Sometimes my mind is not 110 percent there, when he wants to talk to me about a project or whatever it is, because of the cases that I am doing. That is the reason why I have become more selective about the cases that I take now. Sometimes I turn away cases just because I can foresee the headache and the stress that will come with it. Even though they are willing to pay a nice retainer for the case, I won't take it.

Being able to choose her clients is a definite benefit for Vy after her experience as in-house counsel. When working with "bad" clients, it affects her peace of mind and, therefore, the peace of mind she has with her son. Despite the drawbacks, Vy thinks the law is a good profession for a mom:

> Overall, the profession is ideal because it has its flexibility. You can have your own office, make your own set hours, and make as much money as you want. I think it is a good profession, as long as you are conscientious about who you work for and what clients you work with.

Vy has seen some of her legal mom peers leave the profession because of the pressure and guilt resulting from being away from their kids. They are not leaving because they aren't good lawyers but because they feel their pursuit of a career in the legal profession is affecting the welfare of their children. From Vy's perspective, the law could do a better job of allowing women to balance career and motherhood:

> Employers need to create environments conducive to helping mothers feel like they don't have to detrimentally sacrifice one or the other, so they don't feel like they have to choose.

Vy knows that she would pursue a less-demanding career if she felt that her son needed more attention, but he is excelling and she has a terrific support system to make it all work.

> **Advice: Share stories about "legal motherhood."**

In Vy's opinion, legal moms need to share their stories about how they are balancing work and family. Role models have been critical to her success in the law. She credits law professors, colleagues, and judges as women who inspire her every day on her own journey. All of her role models have been strong women who were unconventional in their own way. Vy also recognizes her mother as a tremendous source of strength. Her mother came to the United States after losing her own family in the Vietnam War. Her tenacity and strength has been a roadmap for Vy. The women that Vy hopes to emulate are strong, happy, have balanced lives, and exemplify that anything is possible.

Vy truly believes that motherhood has enhanced her career. It has made her more understanding, and she can visually see what her clients are going through. This sense of clarity has given her insight into their struggles. Motherhood has also made her work harder.

> Motherhood makes you see life differently. It makes you feel like you are working toward something big being a mom because you want your kids to be better off than you were.

She is aware of her responsibility to be a role model to her son, so she talks to him about her cases and her work. It has brought them closer. He wants to grow up to be a lawyer:

> It's allowed me to share my aspirations and achievements with him. It is setting this bar for my son. I can see him taking advantage of the resources that I have made possible for him.

Vy is also tenacious about managing Mikey's life because she wants him to achieve success. She knows how important it is for him to be in a good school. He is an honor role student and on the student council. She acknowledges her Vietnamese culture as instilling these values in her:

> In the Vietnamese culture, family values are number one, especially being a good mother. . . . Instilling educational values is also one of the biggest things in Vietnamese culture.

In addition to learning the Vietnamese language, Mikey is also learning Spanish, as he is Latino from his father's heritage.

Vy also notes that she has had to maintain her own strength because she is a single mom. In her words, "No obstacle is as insurmountable as single motherhood." In Vy's opinion, our culture has moved past the point where single motherhood is stigmatizing. Her family law clients actually feel more at ease with her because she has been in their shoes.

> Being a single mom, it somehow makes you stronger every day, because you know that there is no crutch, so you have to keep working at it. As long as you love what you do as a lawyer and you love being a mom, it all balances out.

It would be an understatement to say that Vy has a lot of energy and the drive to pursue her dreams. She is careful to surround herself with positive and happy people and keeps a safe distance from negative people who might discourage her. She notes, "At thirty-three, I feel more energetic than I have ever felt. I feel more energetic than I felt at twenty-two." As she is dipping her toes into legal academia and is in the beginning stages of a run for political office, Vy will need all the energy she can get.

Last year, Vy began teaching Legal Research and Writing at the Center for Advanced Legal Studies and loves the insight, energy, and practical perspective her students bring to the classroom. On teaching, she comments, "I really find it as an escape and it enhances my legal career." She will soon be expanding her repertoire teaching Business Law at the University of St. Thomas in Houston, Texas. As she does guest speaking at her alma mater, Thurgood Marshall School of Law, she has been approached about teaching there in the future as well.

In the past several months, Vy has also made the decision to run for state representative for Texas House District 26. Although she had an interest in politics, her decision to run for office was predicated by a chance meeting on behalf of a client. Vy represented a restaurant owner who needed to move locations. She had a meeting about retail space with a prominent businessman, who also happened to be the only Vietnamese state representative in Texas. It was well known that he had run in a challenging race, winning by only 33 votes. As she went into his office, she was struck by a picture of the House chamber at the State Capitol in Austin. He told Vy some of his political stories and encouraged her to get involved. He persuaded her to attend an upcoming legislative meeting where she met the chair of the Texas Democratic Party. It was clear from their meeting that they wanted her to seriously consider running for state office. To further push her, the Republican incumbent decided not to seek reelection.

Vy recently announced her candidacy, and her son gave the kick-off speech at her event. She will be running in the primary in March and will be on the ballot with Barack Obama in November 2012.

Advice: Don't let anything hold you back.

In the end, nothing has held Vy Nguyen back—not single motherhood nor negative people who told her that she couldn't do it. She has demonstrated that not only can she have a successful legal career but she can also find fulfillment beyond the law in politics and academics.

However, her greatest joy still comes from her role as a mom. In speaking about her son, Vy makes it clear, "He is the biggest achievement of my life." He has surpassed every expectation she has had. He is a well-balanced child, no matter the circumstances. From Vy's perspective, you don't have to be conventional to succeed in law, in politics, or in life. She is carving out success on her own terms as a legal mom.

Part Six

THE ROAD LESS TRAVELLED

Chapter Seventeen

THE LATE
VOCATION LAWYER

"Don't ever let anybody tell you that you can't, and don't ever let anybody tell you that it is easy. You can and it's not. You can do them both, and you can do them both well."
—*Kathleen Havener*

IN 1960 WHILE OTHER LITTLE GIRLS DREAMED of growing up to become princesses or brides, six-year-old Kathleen Havener dreamed of being a forensic pathologist or a coroner, with the option of being a Congresswoman by the time she was 30. Her father was a general practice physician who often took Kathleen and any number of her eight siblings on rounds at the hospital. She witnessed her first birth when she was six years old. At seven, she attended her first autopsy overseen by a physician who was also a family friend. Even as a child, it was clear that Kathleen was not typical.

Through her college years at the University of Alabama, she maintained a 4.0 grade point average. During her senior year she applied to medical school and began zeroing in on what specialty most interested her, narrowing it down to obstetrics and pathology. At this point, she sought advice from her father on her future, which proved to be a critical crossroads for her. When she approached her father, he replied in his Southern drawl, "Darling, you can't go to medical school; you might take the place of some young man who has to support his family." Being ever the dutiful Irish Catholic daughter, Kathleen abandoned her medical school dream and focused her future toward being a wife and a mother.

She married her college sweetheart who was pursuing law school, eventually specializing in admiralty law, as they lived in Mobile, Alabama, not far from the coast. Kathleen threw herself into motherhood, raising three daughters. She attended PTA meetings, packed lunches, ran a household, and in her spare time became a mega-long-distance runner, a champion quilter, and a pilot. She had not just kinetic energy but also some kind of power that she had to exercise. Kathleen was clearly someone who did not allow the grass to grow under her feet.

She enjoyed intellectual challenges and took on the role of managing her husband's law practice, which he shared with four attorneys. Kathleen had learned legal research and writing at his elbow while he was in law school competing as a finalist in his school's moot court competition. Wrapped up in the competition, he essentially taught her how to help, because otherwise she would never see him. One particular evening in the library after reading all of the copies of *Newsweek*, she approached him and said, "Show me how to do this so we can get out of here." She became his right-hand woman—typing briefs while he dictated, correcting grammar and spelling along the way. It was a team effort.

While he was a second-year student, Kathleen had even taken the LSAT and earned a very respectable score, despite taking the test with a hangover and no real intention to go to law school. She would have been a first-year student while her husband was a third-year student. Ultimately, she did not have the passion for it at the time and decided to focus on their family.

Despite working part time for the law practice, Kathleen was at the helm of a traditional family, with mom handling the kids and the home and dad supporting the family. After a few years, he approached her with an idea. He was concerned that he would not be able to sustain a practice in admiralty law and wanted a second profit center. Would she consider going to law school so they could have two attorney incomes in the event his practice lost strength? After some consideration, but ever the dutiful wife, Kathleen agreed, under one condition—she could choose to go to any law school that she wanted, and her husband would pay for it. He agreed, as this decision coincided with his victory in a large plaintiff's case. She began researching schools within a two-to-four hour radius: Tulane, University of Alabama, Loyola of New Orleans, and Florida State University.

> Advice: Don't be afraid to follow your dreams.

And then she took the LSAT again . . . and received a score one point away from perfect. Twelve years after taking the test for the first time, she had different expectations for herself and untapped ambition. With her daughters aged seven, four and almost three, she sent off applications to Stanford, University of Chicago, Harvard, and Yale. With her LSAT score and perfect college grades, each school accepted her.

She chose Harvard, not only for its reputation for academic excellence but also because she felt that Boston and its surrounding areas were conducive to her family life. In searching for a rental home, they were disheartened to learn that rent in the Boston area was to be six times their mortgage in Alabama. During a house-hunting trip, they stopped for lunch in the North End. Kathleen was crying and said to her husband, "We just can't afford this. We'll have to go back to the original plan." This meant giving up on Harvard and staying in Alabama.

In contemplating the move to Boston, they had decided that he was to be a stay-at-home dad while she attended law school. Her husband came up with the idea of getting a job. Kathleen didn't think it was feasible. They were from Alabama, and Harvard lawyers were a dime a dozen in Boston. He went into his pitch at the table. He wanted to be in Boston for only three years, wanted a high senior associate salary, had no expectations of partnership, and knew admiralty law backward and forward. His extensive trial experience meant that he could take a case on Wednesday and go to trial on Friday. At that moment, someone got up from another table, handed him a card, and asked for his resume. Although he had not been actively searching for a position, he interviewed the next day and had an offer. They moved in May, even though Kathleen wasn't starting school until September. This encounter convinced Kathleen that it was all meant to be.

They moved their girls, then eight, five, and four from Mobile to Lexington, Massachusetts, and began the transition from a "traditional" family with a stay-at-home mom to a family with two parents working outside of the home. Their move was positive in many unforeseen ways. Kathleen realized that she had not wanted to raise her children in Alabama, hoping to expose them to a wider world. Lexington was ethnically and culturally diverse with excellent public schools.

In 1986 at the age of thirty-two, Kathleen loved law school. In her words, law school was "proof of the existence of God." After changing diapers and picking up Cheerios® for several years, having a "job" that required to her to read and think about important and interesting issues was a dream come true. An experience so grounded in intellect was life changing for her. For Kathleen, who had been among the brightest of any classroom she entered, it was the first time she was among a group where she felt her intelligence was middle of the road. An interesting side note, Barack Obama was a classmate, and she sat next to him in one of her classes. She describes him as "spectacularly brilliant."

In Mobile, she was one of only two people who subscribed to *The Economist*. She found that at Harvard Law, the students were interested in big-picture issues as she was. As she participated in a discussion in the Harkness Commons about Salman Rushdie and *The Satanic Verses*, she wept openly because she was so thrilled to be speaking with people who cared about the same issues she did.

How was she able to compete with traditional-aged Harvard Law students for whom sleep was optional and studying was of the ultimate importance? Being a mom of three daughters, Kathleen had exemplary time-management skills. She learned how to do things in a way so that her attention was undivided when she was giving it.

> Advice: Establish a reasonable schedule that allows for family time.

Kathleen's family initially employed a full-time, live-in nanny while she attended school. During the week, she managed her schoolwork as if it were a job. From 8:30 until 5:30 each day, she attended class or studied in the library. She commuted via bus and train most days, arriving home at 6:30. She then cooked dinner for the family, and they sat down together between 7:00 and 7:30. She worked on homework with the girls, until everyone went to bed at 9:30.

Every Saturday, with the exception of the two weeks before exams, was spent with her children. They relished this time as a family, seeking out fun activities like canoeing, apple picking, and college football games. On Sundays, she studied at home, but she was available. Kathleen usually cooked a traditional Sunday dinner. It took a while, but eventually classmates from Harvard joined them on Sunday nights. Their first Thanksgiving in Boston, she invited the students in her section who could not afford to go home to dinner. They watched football games, played in the snow, and enjoyed the company of a home with growing children.

All three of her first semester professors were either her age or younger than she was. Kathleen looked at the issues in her classes from a mature perspective. Five weeks into her Contracts class, they were studying an output and requirements case that dealt with tomatoes. On one side of the case was a large tomato cannery, and on the other was a simple tomato farmer—a classic David and Goliath law school scenario. Most of her classmates felt a liquidation clause in a contract between a poor farmer and a large cannery was ridiculous.

The professor was clearly trying to challenge them toward a particular point, and with moments left in the hour, the students were gearing to get across the courtyard to their next class. Undaunted, Kathleen raised her hand and said not quite eloquently, "I don't really know how to say this, but what about the spaghetti sauce?" This apparently brought down the house in the classroom—students were howling with laughter. The professor turned to her and said, "No matter how inarticulately the question was phrased, you hit upon precisely the point of this case." The following day, he explained the simple chain of events that led from tomato farmer, to cannery, to sauce distributor, to grocery store, to Kathleen, to her children's dinner plates, and how any break in that chain would elicit some form of damage.

This particular professor came back to her on numerous occasions, stressing that she had the intellect and shouldn't be afraid to use it. Her point of view was valued, and her stage of life and experience gave her actual advantages over other students. This professor chose her as a research assistant during the summer after her first year over numerous applicants to assist in editing his tenure piece.

Kathleen never felt that she shortchanged her children by her decision to pursue a career in the law but rather that by seeing her pursue her dreams, they felt liberated to pursue their own dreams. There were some unavoidable consequences of their move away from the South: leaving family, good friends, and especially their trusted housekeeper who had become like a member of their family. These changes were difficult for her daughters, but at this point Kathleen has the perspective of hindsight. She is able to see that although her daughter might have been sad when Mom wasn't home after preschool, as a grown woman, her daughter turned out okay.

She had to make peace with relinquishing the traditional mother role—the way that she herself was raised. It was a sacrifice for Kathleen not to see her children as much as she would have liked as they grew up. Had she remained in Mobile and raised her children, she would have been involved in 80 percent of their upbringing. Their father would have been somewhat involved but not as instrumental as he became when their roles expanded. Her children became comfortable calling their dad when they fell down and skinned their knees.

> Advice: Don't be intimidated, women have important things to say.

For the most part, her classmates and professors were supportive. She had some confrontations with professors where she reminded them that although she might "talk slow," she didn't "think slow." On one particular occasion as a third-year student, she arrived to class two minutes late. As to not disrupt the class, she settled into the back row rather than her assigned seat in the front row. Unfortunately (for him), this particular professor chose that day to single her out, asking her to please take her seat.

Already flustered from her hectic morning and commute, Kathleen walked to the front of the classroom and stood at her assigned seat refusing to sit down. At that point the professor said, "Do you have something to say?" The entire class held its breath, because they *knew* she would have something to say. Kathleen replied,

> Professor, you don't know me. I know that you have come from a very prestigious position in the government. But I am 36 years old and I pay, when you count it all up, $75,000 a year to come to this school. I don't know what you did this morning before you got here, but I know what about 90 percent of the people in this room did. They

crawled out of their beds within the last twenty minutes, they washed their face if we're lucky, they brushed their teeth if we're lucky, they maybe even took a shower and they still got here. I got up, washed my face, brushed my teeth, took a shower, washed my hair, washed three children's hair, did six loads of laundry, fixed six lunches, one for the nanny, had a knock-down, drag out fight with my husband in the car, took the train, got out of the train, ran across campus, fell down twice in the snow, and I am still here two minutes after 8:30 and you have decided to make a mockery of me, because you think it is fun. Well, let me tell ya, you work for me. I am paying a full ride. Nobody is paying for me to go here, except me and my husband. You are not here to chide me. You are not here to correct me. You are not here to make me look like a fool. You are here to do a job. And if somebody weren't paying for you to do that, you wouldn't have one. And I am one of those people paying. So would you mind just not making fun of me again. Oh, and I forgot to mention, I'm prepared.

At the end of her speech, she sat down. The professor had sat down halfway through her speech, but she had not taken her eyes off him. He stood up, walked over to her and said, "My name is Charles Fried. I am the former solicitor general of the United States. Everything you said was appropriate, and every single thing you said was something I needed to be reminded of, and I am so grateful." Her fire and his graciousness earned the respect of the entire class.

Upon graduating from Harvard, Kathleen accepted a job clerking for the DC Court of Appeals, thereby moving the family from Massachusetts to Maryland. For her, clerking was the best legal job in the world, allowing her to research, write, and use her intellectual prowess. It was at this point that it became evident that the family was now following the trajectory of her career.

After her clerkship she took a position with a Washington, DC law firm, which was at that time the largest firm in the world. She describes the firm as incredibly foresighted in dealing with work-life balance issues with a touch of "don't ask, don't tell." By the time she had been there two years, even her youngest child was allowed to ride the DC redline subways by herself. The children would go straight to the subway from school, check in with her at the office, and then explore the museums that were within a few blocks of her office. Sometimes two of the children would head off to a museum, and one of the girls would nap in her office. She simply closed the door and did not openly discuss it.

Over the years, she dealt with any number of issues while trying to advance her career while putting her children first. Years into her law practice, one of her daughters experienced separation anxiety, precipitated by the death of her grandparents and observing other family illnesses. She did not want Kathleen to be out of her presence, and the pain she was experiencing was visible. Forcing her to separate against her will and making her go to school was an extremely difficult process. However, Kathleen was always accessible to her children. Even in law school, Kathleen had a beeper by which the children could page her as needed.

> **Advice: Encourage your children to follow their dreams.**

As a mother, it is clear that Kathleen was comfortable allowing her children to spread their wings. Her children travelled abroad as teens, and generally chased their dreams. In Kathleen's opinion, in order to be a successful, accomplished woman, one has to cross borders or boundaries in whatever way possible. In her case, she crossed the Mason-Dixon Line to a new career and life. She encouraged this same spirit of adventure in her daughters.

During the time she was working in Washington, DC, she and her husband made the decision to divorce. Their divorce had nothing to do with their careers but precipitated from irreconcilable differences related to personal issues. They continued to co-parent their children, who were then teenagers or pre-teenaged.

Later in her career, Kathleen, then working at another large firm, was assigned to a long-term case in Alaska. As she made the temporary move to Alaska, her now ex-husband took over her lease in DC and moved in with the girls. The firm had a policy whereby they would pay for "significant others" to visit attorneys on long-term assignments. Kathleen informed the firm that she had three "significant others" and that she would like each daughter to visit her in Alaska during her assignment. The partners in charge of the decision went into an interpretive session to decide whether this was appropriate. Kathleen interrupted the session, saying, "You have got to be kidding me. You are spending way more than it would cost to send my three daughters to Alaska for a week. You don't have to pay for food or a hotel room. You just have to pay for one-round trip flight for each kid, and you are doing it for lots of people who aren't married to their partners. Are you actually going to have twenty partners sit in a room to decide if my children are "significant others"? The partners came to their senses and said, "Of course" and paid for her daughters to visit—yet another example of a barrier that Kathleen was unafraid to break.

Motherhood is an unceasing job, even when children are grown adults. Interestingly, Kathleen felt that she experienced raised eyebrows from firm partners when she insisted on taking time off to visit her daughters after they had their own children, even when she was an income partner herself who was self-governed.

Recently while Kathleen was watching the movie *March of the Penguins* she became emotional, thinking about how her children are grown and all of the things they went through as a family. The movie was particularly poignant as it chronicles how penguins protect their young until they are self-sufficient. Perhaps her strong reaction to the movie demonstrates a subconscious unresolved dilemma that many working mothers cannot avoid: missing a part of their children's upbringing in order to fulfill their own professional aspirations.

Although her daughters spread their wings earlier than Kathleen expected, Kathleen marvels at the accomplishments of each of her daughters who have carved out their own careers—one as a teacher in the Civil Service in France, one pursuing a PhD in Cultural Anthropology, and one practicing as a nurse. They inspire her pride, admiration, and wonder. She feels her own educational accomplishments inspired them.

As a woman who did not pursue motherhood and a legal career completely simultaneously, but in some ways sequentially, Kathleen offers the following advice to women who want to practice law and have a family:

- Be open-minded to life but not so open minded that your brain falls out. Your kids will challenge you every day. Your law career will challenge you every day. You have to meet all of the challenges and keep your sense of humor.
- Be flexible so that if you have been open-minded and your children change their minds, it is all right.
- It is always going to be all right. It is all worth it. Even the hard days.

- Read everything Deborah Tannen ever wrote. She is a linguistics scholar from Georgetown University who has written extensively on conversational discourse between men and women. Her work inspired Kathleen to have conversations with her own adolescents when they were both facing the same way—driving in the car, pretending to watch television, etc. This advice proved incredibly helpful during the teen years.
- Use technology. Connecting with children can be accomplished through more than face-to-face communication.

In addition to these five rules, the MOST important piece of advice Kathleen offers is to BE KIND: to your children, to yourself, to your colleagues, to opposing counsel and parties, and to everyone you meet. This is the easiest to forget as demands pile up and life gets increasingly stressful.

Kathleen has remarried and relocated to Ohio where she now shares a law practice with her husband. She speaks as someone who is proud of her life and unafraid of the challenges to come.

Kathleen remarked, "I was afraid of everything until I was in my thirties, until I realized I was a nut. I was a complete lunatic." By facing up to the challenges of a legal career and raising children, Kathleen unlocked her own power and has become fulfilled in her career and life.

Chapter Eighteen

THE PART-TIME LEGAL MOM AND THE FAMILY FIRM

"It is the most difficult time of my life. It is the most rewarding, but it is also the most difficult."
—*Maureen Pikarski*

MAUREEN PIKARSKI'S LIFE is rooted in family and the law. She remarks, "Law has always been a part of our lives." As a part-time legal mom working for her father's law practice in Chicago, she spends her workdays with her father, two brothers, and husband at the family firm. On the days she is at home, she manages the activities of four children under the age of five, including a set of twins.

Maureen always felt she would follow her father's footsteps into the field of law. Observing him practice with his partner of forty-five years, she comments, "It was so much of our life. . . . I admired what he did. He worked hard and I admired that. So that is what I wanted to do. He seemed to enjoy it. That was always really my direction."

Maureen completed an undergraduate degree from Bryn Mawr College, an all women's college. She very much values her experience at Bryn Mawr:

It was a very positive experience. I was really challenged as a woman—female role models constantly reminding you of all of the women achievers out there. I think that is maybe the starting ground for having kept me going as opposed to just saying, "I don't want to deal with it. I am just going to be a stay-at-home mom." You were really challenged to pursue things and not to shy back because you are the only female around. . . . Being at a woman's college was definitely beneficial.

Maureen subsequently graduated with a master's degree in International Studies at Villanova University. Though she thought that she would eventually pursue law school, her enviable first job was with the White House Office of Public Liaison during the first Clinton administration. Maureen specifically worked in the Public Outreach Office. She really enjoyed this position and the importance that the administration placed on public outreach. Maureen worked on both business and ethnic outreach. During her two and a half years in the office, she was thrilled to have the opportunity to work on exciting projects including the Pope's visit to the United States.

At a certain point, she felt it might be time for her to make a change, knowing that she eventually wanted to move back to Chicago and start a legal career. Her father also indicated that there was an opening for another attorney in the office. Maureen was able to continue her work at the White House on part-time basis while she attended law school at Catholic University. After graduation, she joined her father's firm specializing in real estate taxation and zoning law.

Initially, the firm consisted of her father, his partner, and Maureen. She learned the intricacies of property tax law and proved to be a valuable asset to the firm. Eventually one of her brothers joined the firm, then another, and finally her husband came on board once Maureen changed to a part-time schedule.

Although Maureen and her husband knew that they wanted a family, they were married for five years before having children. Professionally, her life was on track. She was able to work nights and weekends. She relates, "Part of being a lawyer is networking. A lot of those events were at night." As a couple, they were both able to dedicate themselves to their careers and able to make a significant amount of money working.

With her career in full swing, Maureen and her husband decided it was time to start a family. Despite reports in magazines about women having children at advanced ages, Maureen knew that her biological clock was ticking if she wanted to have kids. She notes, "One of the things women have to deal with is age." After having her first child, she welcomed her second child only fourteen months later and twins the following year. In less than four years, she had gone from a relatively unencumbered career woman to a mother with four children.

> Advice: Keep your career active.

After her second child arrived, Maureen made the decision to go to a part-time schedule. The firm was very supportive, and she describes her father as being "very sympathetic" to her new responsibilities. Maureen was determined to continue working, knowing how detrimental career gaps can be to women:

> If you do want to keep your career, you do have to keep it active while you are having a family. The legal profession is not one you can sit out and go back even two years later. Even if it is volunteer work, try to do something to keep your resume active during that time. If you are going to choose to pull back or stay at home, you need to do something because you can't go back and pick it up.

Maureen was fortunate that the firm cooperated with her new schedule, structuring her time so that she was given work rather than leading a case. Her husband also joined the firm, alleviating some of the burden. In her particular practice area, real estate taxation, work can be brought home and can even be done after the kids go to sleep. In her current circumstances, she is not required to have much client contact.

> Advice: Know your priorities.

The change from being a senior attorney at the firm with fifteen years of experience to having work given to her was a hard transition, especially as that work was dictated by her younger brothers and her dad. In her words, she went "from leading the case, to being told what to do." Maureen naturally wants to take over and organize cases, but she has to sit back because of the choice she has made to work part time. Although this has been an "ongoing struggle," Maureen has defined her priorities:

> At some point, it just has to be. You have to be realistic with what you can do. There is no supermom. You can't do both well; you have to make sacrifices. I want to stay at the firm. I want to practice.

Currently, Maureen works about thirty hours a week. She is in the office two days a week and works from home one day a week. With four children under the age of five, she has a lot of support to make this work, commenting, "In order to do all this, you have to have a great support structure."

Maureen's husband is very supportive. Though he works full time at the firm, he is very helpful at home. He knows that based on the ages of their children, they often need two adults to see to all of the children's needs at the end of the day. It certainly helps that he loves being involved with the kids and their family life.

In addition, Maureen has both a babysitter who comes to her home and her mother lives nearby to help with school shuttling. When she is working from her home office, she closes the door and the babysitter knows not to disturb her. She will have lunch with the kids and take breaks for school drop off and pick up. She tries to accomplish as much as she can at the office and during the work day, as working at night can be difficult when she is exhausted after putting in a full day:

> You have to be organized and disciplined. Because you can't put it off. I am not the type of person who can stay up until two in the morning and then get up at six to start my day again. I just try to be organized and get as much done as I can. When I am at work, I will stay there as long as I can. I will be there from 7:00 a.m. to 7:00 p.m. to make the most of my day.

To Maureen, the biggest benefit of working part time is that she is able to be an integral part of her children's lives. She was reluctant to put the kids in daycare, and she wanted to be with them. As a couple, when Maureen and her husband decided to have a family, they knew that they didn't want a nanny raising them but wanted to be responsible for raising their own kids. Incidentally, Maureen lives in the same neighborhood where she grew up and has chosen to send the kids to the same school she attended.

Having a part-time schedule also allows Maureen to have some of the benefits of work, beyond just a paycheck. She is able to engage in intellectually stimulating work. She can get dressed up and feel like a human being part of the larger world. As many working moms know, sometimes it can feel good to get away.

On the other hand, working part time necessitates a delicate balance between being a mom and an attorney. It can be difficult to switch from one mindset to the other:

> For me it is hard to transition from day to day. One day you're a lawyer, the next day you're a mom. It is really hard to make that transition from day to day. So I try to get as much done on both ends. When I am with the kids, I try to block out work as much as I can, and given the nature of the business, I can. I check my voicemail, but I don't have to have access to clients at that time. If there is an emergency, somebody can contact me, but otherwise, it is really just family time during the time that I am off. When I am at work, . . . I trust the babysitter that I have.

In addition, working part time has resulted in Maureen sacrificing her professional advancement. She simply cannot dedicate the time that some of her peers can at this point in her life. Maureen relates:

> The hardest thing is seeing some of my peers advance and I am not because of my choice to go part time and to have a family. That is hard when you are with your peers and you see them talking about promotions, or going to events, or nabbing that client because they were able to work and get that client. I am envious at times because I can't do it. I don't want to do it. That is just my choice to be part time and to try to balance the two as best as I can. There has to be give and take.

Despite cutting down her hours and sacrificing some of her professional aspirations, Maureen still feels like she is shortchanging her kids by having a career. In her words, "You cannot do both well. You are one person." Even with her reduced hours, her kids sometimes cry when she has to leave for the office. Maureen would like to do more with her children; however, like any working parent, she is tired at the end of the day and can be short with the kids as a result. Essentially, she tries to pay attention to what she really wants for her family and focuses on how she wants to raise her kids. On the days that she is able, she does a lot with the kids: museums, classes, and at-home projects. In the back of her mind, she knows that she could be doing even more if she was at home with them full time. She simply feels torn between both lives.

At its core, to Maureen being a mom "is extremely fulfilling." She particularly enjoys seeing how nice her four kids are to each other. Maureen also loves their intellectual curiosity and watching them grow as individuals with specific interests. The fact that the kids are growing up closely in age is an added bonus, because they have similar interests. Having a large family within such a short span of time is a challenge in itself, but Maureen would not do anything differently:

> I am really happy with the way things are. . . . It would have been easier to space the kids out as opposed to having four kids within three years. But on the other hand, that would have caused me to pull back on work sooner.

Reflecting on this time of her life, Maureen remarks how people say, "How cute, you have twins." With four children under the age of five, the reality is that someone always needs her attention. In response to these demands, Maureen simply explains, "You find the strength."

As Maureen is part of a family of lawyers working together, it is interesting to compare their relative situations. Her father has always practiced full time, and Maureen's mother stayed at home to raise the children. Her brother works full time, but his wife stays at home and manages the home front. Over the years, he has adapted his hours to accommodate family concerns, arriving to the office earlier in order to leave earlier and limiting work on the weekends. Maureen's youngest brother is single and can devote more time to his career. Although Maureen is envious of his ability to prioritize work, she knows that she really cannot compare the two situations.

As law is the family business, it would be natural for Maureen to encourage her own children to follow in her footsteps. However, she would encourage her children to look further, knowing the realities of the legal profession:

> I will steer them in a different direction. I think the legal profession is flooded with attorneys. I think there is a certain glamour to it that is not the reality. I would have them explore other things first to allow for creativity. I like the idea that my dad started a firm, and it is his

business. But I think the legal profession is a very tough profession. Dealing with clients is extremely difficult, being dependent on them. I would really steer them in a different direction.

Moreover, Maureen generally does not think the law is a good career for a mom, unless a woman carves out a niche for herself in a practice area that is accommodating to family concerns. In her opinion, the law "is just very demanding." She has had success working part time and has seen colleagues with manageable careers working in-house as corporate counsel. Maureen cautions, "Litigation is not family friendly in any way." She counsels that it is even tough on a family when the husband is a litigator and the wife is a stay-at-home mom. Bolstering her opinion that the law is not necessarily a favorable career for moms, Maureen also comments on the gender disparity in the profession:

> It is very much still a boys' club. Maybe that will change as there are now more women in law school. . . . Especially in the area that I am in, it is still very male dominated. I will go to court, and I will be the only female there. . . . It is not very kind to women.

In order for the legal profession to be a better workplace for working mothers, Maureen notes, "There would have to be more flexibility." At many large firms, attorneys who are not performing optimally because of family concerns or other reasons can be replaced readily because there are other attorneys lined up at the door to take their place. In order to survive at a large firm, an attorney has to be so valuable that the firm finds them irreplaceable. This can be difficult for anyone with competing responsibilities beyond work. Regardless, Maureen has seen progress with more women entering the profession and corporations becoming more conscious of the importance of hiring attorneys with an awareness toward gender and minority issues. She notes that moving forward, women need to support each other in order to advance within the profession:

> Any progress is good progress, but it is going to take a long time. Maybe with more women in the profession, it will change. Women also need to stick together. You can't have a partner woman not being sympathetic or a woman who does not have kids not being sympathetic toward someone who does. Women really need to stick together

themselves—those that are in a leadership position need to help those who are trying to work their way up. I don't know if we are doing such a good job of that.

Advice: Plan your career carefully.

With this in mind, Maureen advises women to think carefully about their legal careers. She notes, "First of all, find a field that is friendlier to families and women and also a place that allows flexibility too." When looking for a job, consider practice areas that will be supportive of family life. In-house positions, government counsel, and even teaching law might be more conducive to raising children as opposed to a career in litigation. She also advises that it can be hard to transition in one's career, so it is important to find the right fit early, noting, "It is hard to change paths if you get too far into your career."

Advice: Talk to other women who have good situations.

Maureen also recommends talking to other women in the profession who appear to have good work-life situations. She was able to observe not only her own colleagues but her father's peers and her brother's peers as she grew within the profession, noting what might work for her own family life. She was able to see women with great professional lives whose personal lives suffered. There is no one-size fits all. In her words, "Observe the women around you . . . and see what in your heart is good for you, and make decisions based on that."

Ultimately, Maureen would like to build a life that satisfies both her professional and personal goals. Professionally, she would like to be recognized for her work:

> I would like to be a successful real estate tax attorney—somebody who is prominent in the field of real estate taxation, an expert in the area. I like what I am doing. I would like to stick with it.

As her children get older and become more independent, she may need to spend more time working in order to reach her goals. However, she will always find a way to balance both worlds because in her words,

"Family is what you've got at the end of the day." In regard to her personal life, she hopes . . .

> to have a good marriage and have four happy, well-adjusted, interesting kids who take part in life. I think there is so much out there to be learned and enjoyed, that they experience things. They can then decide what they like and don't like, but to experience things.

Like any working parent, Maureen worries about whether her children will feel neglected by her dual-focus on home and career. However, she hopes that they will see that there is another aspect to her—that they might see her professional accomplishments. In juggling both a career and home life, she aspires to be a role model for her children, especially for her daughter.

To many women, Maureen depicts the perfect blend of work-life balance, having a successful career on a part-time basis and the ability to have an integral role in raising her children. Maureen rejects the notion that anyone can really have it all, noting that women have to look beyond impossible standards:

> Be realistic. In my opinion, and I have a lot of friends in the legal profession, you can't have it all. It is impossible. From the people I know, nobody has it all. There is going to be give and take. Think about what you want your family life to be and what you want your children to be like and whether you want to have a role in raising them or not.

For now, being a part-time lawyer has allowed Maureen the flexibility to manage her home life and the ability to carry on her career. Though no situation is perfect, it is working for her and her family:

> For me, the part-time approach really works. It is kind of a happy medium, or maybe an unhappy medium. Nobody is really happy, but it works. I really think it is a good option for women.

Chapter Nineteen

THE WAY WE WERE

"It might not be the career you thought you were going to have, or it might not be the career you started to have. It might be a better one in some ways, a different one in others. You are not locked in to one choice."
—Alice Bruno

GROWING UP IN THE 1960S, Alice Bruno was so committed to not having children that she told her high school boyfriend that she had no desire to procreate. She received very clear messages throughout her childhood that being a professional while having a family was not possible. As the youngest child and only daughter of four, both of Alice's parents reinforced that she could do and be anything. In addition, her mother told her that having children and staying home would be entirely unsatisfying and that she should focus on a career. While at boarding school, a classmate's mother who was a doctor spoke to the students and emphatically said that women could not be mothers and professionals (despite the fact that she had a teenage daughter and was a physician). Alice chose her path, and it was not the archetypical 1950s wife and mother.

She decided to attend Tufts University, partially because she felt that they had a terrific record of educating women. She chose to major in English and Social Psychology. In the mid-1970s, most of her professors were men; however, Alice had a wonderful experience at Tufts.

There were gender issues being discussed around the Ivy League at the time. Alice was just becoming aware of such issues, having attended all girls' schools up to that point.

She entered the University of Connecticut School of Law in 1977. During her first year, she became disillusioned with law. She simply didn't feel like the students or professors were talking about how cases impacted people. Her interests leaned toward social service, so Alice decided to enroll in the joint JD/Master's in Social Work program. Through this program, she was able to include a substantive area concentration in women's issues as part of her curriculum.

Overall, Alice had a positive experience in law school. Her law school class was generally split between men and women. She recounts one adjunct professor telling students that women should take care because juries might think a female attorney had a weaker case than her male adversary did at trial. One of her clinical professors stressed that the most important quality in being a good lawyer was being yourself. Alice took this advice to heart, especially as she became a legal mom years later.

She was at the top of her class academically but sometimes felt behind the curve. She was never approached for the law review and wasn't aware of its importance. Moreover, she didn't realize the significance of securing a judicial clerkship. She generally did not do any summer internships, as she was completing a joint degree.

During her final semester at law school, Alice received several offers from corporations and large law firms. At the time, firms were just becoming aware that they should not ask interview questions about motherhood. At an on-campus interview, Alice felt that the dance around the question of motherhood was very obvious, but she was able to address the issue saying that she had no plans to have children. Alice commented that the women in her class knew of the implications of mentioning children in an interview, and the woman who handled career services had prepped them.

In 1981, Alice chose to join a mid-to-large sized firm in New Haven, Connecticut. She was impressed that they were one of the earliest firms to have a female partner. The firm had a terrific reputation with a long history of commitment to community service and the bar association. Entirely focused on work, she notes, "When I went to work at a law firm, having children was the furthest thing from my mind."

Four years later, now established on partnership track, Alice became anxious about telling the partners at the firm that she was getting married. She still did not see this union as something that might lead to children, but she was concerned that they might not take her as seriously. She was already concerned about gender issues at the firm. In her words, "It was clear to me that I didn't get to try very many cases because I was a girl."

About a year into her marriage, Alice started thinking more about children. Up to that point, she had been resolute in her conviction that she was not going to have children:

> In my mind, it was entirely physiological. I was walking across the New Haven Green and kept seeing all these women with children and thinking, "Why can they have children and I can't?" "Why do they get to have children?" Then I started to realize that I had made this choice. I was also very keenly aware that there was no way that I would be able to work as hard as I wanted to, and as many hours as I wanted to, and become a partner in this law firm, which was very intense, if I were to have a child.

Alice was afraid that having a baby would thwart her chances for partnership. She knew of another woman who had left the firm because she wanted to return to the firm on a part time basis after having her first child. That woman went on to work for a competing law firm that met her accommodation. The overall feeling of the firm was that this woman had let the firm down by leaving after she had a baby.

> By the time I decided I wanted to have kids, I was painfully aware of the fact that I would never dream of having them until I thought I would be a partner and all the cards were on the table that I was going to be a partner.

Despite her fears, her colleagues at the firm were supportive when she told them the news that she was pregnant. Some of the attorneys even offered baby name suggestions. In her words, "I felt like I was part of a family at the firm at that time. I was eager to come back and get back to work and be a real productive partner and assume all of the responsibilities of being a partner."

1987 was a busy year for Alice. By June, she had billed over 1,000 hours. She had just finished her presidency of the New Haven County

Bar Association—Young Attorneys and was beginning her tenure as president of the Connecticut Bar Association—Young Lawyers Division. Her oldest daughter was born in July. She expected to be voted in as a partner at the August/September partnership meeting with her partnership term beginning the following January.

The firm maternity policy was limited to six weeks of disability, with additional time considered on a case-by-case basis considering the needs of the woman and the needs of the firm. The firm did not limit Alice's leave to her period of disability. She chose to take four months off, planning to be back full time in December so that she could receive her annual retirement contribution at the end of the year.

Alice returned to the firm with her daughter in an in-home daycare four days per week and with her husband's mother one day per week. Although she and her husband had planned to switch off picking up her daughter from daycare, the reality was that Alice was called upon to do so most nights. She also was eager to see her daughter at the end of the day.

Alice loved working hard and working a lot. However, she soon felt exhausted with her new responsibilities. By New Year's, she already had pneumonia. Alice blames herself. She loved being a lawyer and found it difficult to manage everything, especially having to scale back her work.

In February of 1988, Alice was asked to sit on a panel at the ABA meeting in Denver titled, "From Diapers to Depositions." The panelists were comprised of Alice, who returned to work full time after having a child, a male attorney with children who chose to work part-time, and a woman who gave up her practice after having children. At that time, Alice was very adamant that she would continue to work full time while she raised her daughter.

Her perspective changed when she and her husband decided to have a second child. It was their hope that the children would be born two years apart; however, things didn't go as planned. In December, Alice suffered a miscarriage. The firm was unaware of her condition. It was very difficult time for Alice:

> It really knocked me for a loop. It was the first time that I hadn't been able to do everything I set my mind to. I felt tremendously guilty that it was my fault because I was working too hard.

With her daughter at eighteen months, and having just lost a baby, Alice wanted to stay home for the week between Christmas and New

Year's. Her husband, also an attorney, cautioned her about whether it was a good idea. Alice credits this period as the beginning of real struggle for her of wanting to be home with her daughter and needing to be at work.

Alice subsequently suffered a second miscarriage and chose to tell her firm about it. She approached the then-managing partner of the firm and asked him if she could work part time on the advice of her doctor. He was not sympathetic and responded by asking, "What, do you have an incompetent cervix?" Despite this partner's insensitive response, it was clear to Alice that with him at the helm, the firm was not willing to revisit the idea of part-time work. They had already turned down a female associate who had asked for a part-time schedule. Alice comments, "By the time it got to me, it was 'You can't be partner and work part time, because as a partner your whole focus is supposed to be the practice of law.'"

Alice took an unpaid three-month leave to focus on getting pregnant and dealing with her home, which was going through major renovations. She returned to the firm in November, pregnant and desperately wanting things to go well. She had a difficult pregnancy, during which her doctor put her on disability for the final three months. Her second daughter was born in June, approximately three years younger than her first daughter.

At this point, the firm told her that she could come back to work whenever she wanted but that she could not come back part time. Part of the problem was that full-time partners for full pay were working the part-time hours that she was proposing. The firm didn't know how it could reconcile the two. Essentially, she was being penalized for being a hard worker. Alice notes that several of her colleagues were outraged by the decision:

> It wasn't a uniform decision, and it wasn't the firm's decision. I didn't have the wisdom to challenge it or say, "Wait a second, I want people to vote on this." . . . At that point, I was just so anxious to be out of there.

Had Alice pushed for a vote on this issue, things might have been different. At the time, she was one of only three female partners at the firm. Alice chose to honor the firm's decision and stayed home for a year with her daughters.

Alice had mixed feelings about being at home full time with her daughters. She felt lost and isolated. With a three year old and an infant, she was unable to multitask the way that she had in the past. She had gone from feeling competent to feeling incompetent.

> I loved being home on many levels, and on other levels it was so hard for me because I had gone from being an intense lawyer . . . and I was stuck in Branford with two little kids and no help. It was really hard.

A year later when the time came to go back to the firm, Alice needed to extend her leave twice to deal with the deaths of her father-in-law and mother. She returned to work in October and describes the next year as the hardest of her life.

They hired an au pair and learned subsequently that the au pair had taken the children in the car to her friend's home without seatbelts, telling the children not to tell their mom. Alice decided to return to a traditional daycare setting. However, with two children, the logistics became more complicated. Her older daughter needed to be picked up from nursery school and transported to the daycare every day at lunchtime. Alice began performing this shuttle service, which became increasingly difficult because her daughter did not want to go to the daycare. Having had Alice home for a year, her daughter wanted to be at home with her. Alice would then return to work and pick up both children by 6:00 each evening.

During this year, Alice notes, "In my mind, I felt like I was neither a good mother nor a good lawyer." Alice was not completely satisfied with her daycare situation. When she went to pick up the kids one day, one of the childcare providers had cut her younger daughter's bangs. This situation coupled with her older daughter hating daycare gave Alice pause. She comments, "Whenever I was at work, I wanted to be at home. Whenever I was at home, I wanted to be at work."

In the fall, Alice learned that she was pregnant with her third child. She tried to keep it a secret for as long as she could, with the knowledge that it could jeopardize her work at the firm. She felt that most people understood when she had one child, even when she didn't want to have an only child and decided to have a second. When she ultimately announced that she was expecting her third, one of the partners who had been supportive to that point said, "Don't you know where babies come from?" This was ironic, as many of her male partners had large families with nary a comment from anyone in the office.

The firm had asked her to train in a new specialty of health care law when she returned after her second pregnancy but changed their minds once she announced that she was having her third child. She had the baby in June and decided she would be back at the firm by the end of the year. Once again, she hoped to negotiate a part-time schedule. The time at home was more important to her than the money. Unfortunately, the deal was the same as it had been—she could take off as long as she wanted, but she had to return to the firm full time. She began to have doubts about whether going back was the best idea.

Advice: Know when to make the tough decisions.

Ultimately, Alice decided to the leave the firm where she had started her legal career. Her husband had started a small legal practice in the town where they lived. He asked her to join him in the "partnership that matters." She decided to make the leap. The new position afforded her the flexibility she needed to be a good mom, but in retrospect Alice was unhappy with her new situation. She was trying to be all things to all people—a great lawyer, a great wife, and a great mom. Alice felt depressed and overwhelmed. She felt that caring for three kids had put her over the edge. She used her entire capital account payout from the firm for babysitters so that she could manage all of her responsibilities.

Leaving the large established firm was a difficult transition for Alice. She was able to take on some interesting cases and probate appointments. Moreover, she became a superior court magistrate, which essentially allowed her to adjudicate small claims and motor vehicle cases for about $150 per day. This was important to her because she wanted to stay in court. Nevertheless, she missed the intensity of being at a large firm in a large city.

She regrets that she is no longer a partner in a large firm and came to resent her husband for not being more supportive in helping her manage their family life. Her career was the more traditionally successful one, and she considers herself more ambitious and aggressive in regard to her career. After eighteen years of marriage and twelve years as law partners, Alice and her husband ultimately chose to divorce.

Alice does not regret the time that she was able to spend with her children by stepping away from large-firm life. She was able to be in their school as a volunteer and was very involved in their day-to-day activities.

With her life in transition and her children well launched, Alice decided to take her career in a new direction by submitting an application for Connecticut Judicial Selection Commission. As she has made it through the application process, she awaits the possibility of a judicial appointment by the governor of Connecticut.

Alice now works as the deputy chief clerk of the New Haven Judicial District. She is reflective about her experience as a legal mom, especially as she mentors young women navigating careers in the law. She admits to feeling conflicted about her feminist ideals. As much as she supports a woman's right to have children, she feels frustrated with young women who are not willing to make the sacrifices she made, especially those who became pregnant having just found their way to the courthouse:

> What mystified me when other women came in after me as associates was that [they] would dream of having a baby until [they] made partner. It truly never occurred to me that if you hadn't put in your dues, if you hadn't proven yourself, if you hadn't reached that level of success in the field that you could dare sidetrack yourself, sidetrack your career to take a maternity leave.
>
> I was trying to be a mentor to young women and they would be coming in and having babies within two years. . . . I remember thinking I am really confused about this—how can I be a feminist and be upset with them for deciding that having babies is more important than having a career? But it was hard. I have to admit it was hard. Because I felt that I had made some serious decisions about the importance of my career.

In her opinion, young women are not conscious of the compromises and sacrifices that they will need to make as legal moms. She expresses dismay at how many women take their husband's last name, rather than keeping their own.

Alice sometimes envies women who have worked their way to top positions in law firms and corporations, especially those who were able to do so who also had children. She acknowledges that she could not "have it all," and maybe no one really can:

I still struggle with the specter that I have failed as a woman lawyer because there are other women my age who have been much more professionally successful who have children who didn't have this kind of disjointed practice that I had.

Advice: Know your priorities and limitations.

Having three children, Alice did not feel that she could manage her intense large law firm career and be the mother that she wanted to be, but it still bothers her sometimes. She says, "Even when you know you have gotten it right for you personally, there is still this little piece of you that thinks maybe I could have done more, maybe I could have been better." In her opinion, there are few women who have had more than one child who have risen to high levels professionally.

I think that some of the women who are a little bit older than me and certainly a lot of women who have achieved greater career success had only one child or had none."

Alice is doubtful that the legal landscape has really changed for working moms since the 1980s. She notes, "This is the real world, and we are in a time when lawyers don't have jobs." She sees fabulous attorneys, both men and women, who are not getting jobs. In her opinion, reality says that if a young man and young woman are both seeking a particular job, the man will have the advantage because he will not be asking for concessions related to parenthood.

I think I am a feminist, but I also feel like the business world is the way it is, and no matter how far we have come, there is a difference between affirmative action and picking between two people, one whom is able to dedicate themselves to the job and one who can't."

In the legal environment, Alice feels that serious lawyers who put in the time and work are going to get ahead over those that want to focus more time and energy on their personal and family lives. However, Alice's critical piece of advice for younger women is that we all have choices. We can choose to spend more time with our children or choose to focus on our careers.

From my perspective, if I have done one thing for younger women is to make sure that they understand that there are choices. That is what I always say to them. . . . You are only taking one day at a time and don't worry. If you decide you are working full time today, it doesn't mean that you have to work full time for the rest of your life. If you decide you are part time today, it doesn't mean you are part time for the rest of your life. If you go home for a few years, you haven't damned yourself to being home.

For Alice, the only choice that is irreversible is whether or not to have children. If you choose to have children, there is no way to avoid making hard decisions. With her daughters now twenty-four, twenty-one, and nineteen, Alice cautions all working moms, including herself, on what *not* to do:

"Don't be so hard on ourselves, and don't see ourselves as failures." If I weren't a successful lawyer, it would have been much harder to be the mom I was and to be the strong woman role model I think I wanted to be for my kids.

Chapter Twenty

PRO BONO LEGAL MOMS

THE WEST COOK PRO BONO NETWORK

*"There's not a lot geared toward keeping people in the profession. . . .
It is hard for me to believe that we as a society don't want
to use that talent—people who take breaks."*

—Donna Peel

IN 2010, DONNA PEEL started looking for a job after taking a planned
break starting in 2003 to raise her children. Having an undergraduate
degree in economics from Michigan State University and a law degree
from Washington University School of Law in St. Louis, Donna's educational background was stellar.

In addition, she had gone to law school specifically to study antitrust law and had worked at the Department of Justice (DOJ) in the
Antitrust Division, in her words, "exactly as I had planned and hoped."
Donna loved her job at the DOJ and had initially thought she would be
a working mom. Around the time her son turned two, she had to make
the difficult decision to stay at home:

> I had never intended, ever in my wildest dreams, ever, to be a stay-at-
> home mother. *Ever.* And I just assumed that I would make this work
> and I would figure out the trick. There were just some competing

interests on my child's welfare side that needed to be attended to. And that combined with the demands of travelling and a husband who worked at a private law firm, it just wasn't working out and didn't make much sense. I took a planned break, hoping it would be very short. Then came the second baby.

When starting her job search, Donna thought her eleven years at the Justice Department in various capacities would put her in good stead as she reentered the workforce after almost eight years at home raising children. She comments, "I just always assumed that I had a very strong resume and great experience and would very easily find a similar job to the one I loved."

Moreover, Donna had kept her mind active during her children's formative years. She had been a member of the local school board and worked on two national campaigns as a policy analyst. The *St. Louis Dispatch* had even quoted some of her research . Donna loved mothering her two children but wanted to engage her mind as well:

> I think I am pretty typical of lawyers who stay at home. You just have to find some sort of fulfillment. Being at home can have its rewards also, but it is a really hard adjustment.

After networking and sending out resumes, Donna got interviews for two jobs, neither of which were entirely great fits for her. However, she was excited about future possibilities. One of her interview questions would prove to be the catalyst for her new calling in life.

In discussing her years away from paid work, the interviewer asked Donna how she had spent her time. She describes the encounter: "During the very last interview at one of the jobs, I was asked, 'You mean, you haven't even done any pro bono work?'" Donna had looked for pro bono work over the years, but as she looked at training opportunities for pro bono, they were set up for traditional office lawyers—mostly during after work or after school hours. Donna started to think about the obvious waste of legal talent due to lawyers taking breaks for their families. She also noted that there were pleas from nonprofits and the bar associations who needed pro bono help:

> Basically, I was interested in doing some pro bono work, but I kept thinking, "There must be a solution to this problem here. I have all these flexible hours from 8:00 to 3:00. I think there must be a solution

for people like me where the commuting is more workable, where the hours make more sense, and take advantage of the hours that I have."

Donna started talking about the issue. From other moms in her situation, she learned that some nonprofits had actually turned down offers to do free work. She also learned that the training hours and locations were generally not convenient. Also, several of the moms had concerns. They wanted to be reliable for the work but also had priorities at home, for example, what were they to do when a child was home sick? Donna also started a dialogue with some of the nonprofit organizations. Though interested in tapping into the talent, it didn't always make sense for them to do individual training for lawyer moms who were taking a break from paid work. Donna decided to tackle this issue: "I found it very difficult to believe that society wanted all of these resources not used to the max. I felt that in not getting a job, there was this feeling, 'Wait a second, are you serious?'"

Donna learned about a group called Chicago Pro Bono Moms, which for geographical reasons would not work for her. However, they referred her to the Public Interest Law Initiative (PILI), a group that immediately understood what she was trying to accomplish. PILI sent her two pages of nonprofit organizations that they felt might be a good fit for her proposed model.

Early in 2011, Donna came up with the idea for the West Cook Pro Bono Network, essentially a group of lawyers banding together to give some time for pro bono causes. Their website states,

> We are a network of attorneys based in Oak Park/River Forest, Illinois who want to give back to the community, but have found limited individual opportunities due to other obligations, be it job or family. As a group, we are better able to arrange projects in a way that are convenient to our hours and structure them so that there is always backup. Our organization is ideal for caregivers since our projects are team or pair-based as well as chosen with sensitivity to geographic location and school-pickup times. All attorneys are welcome. Inactive status is allowed under Illinois rules. Projects are underway with training, occasional CLE, and malpractice insurance provided.

In order to get started, Donna sent out an e-mail through Oak Park Mom Mail, which has thousands of members. She invited anyone interested in learning more about the idea to an informational meeting. On

February 1, 2011, the day of the worst snowstorm in Chicago, ten women met around Donna's kitchen table. She explained the overall idea and set forth several potential projects. They decided as a group on the first two projects.

> **Advice: Start small and choose projects that will succeed.**

Donna found plenty of nonprofits that would have worked for the group, but she was careful initially to pitch projects that allowed the group to see success up front. They committed to Lawyers in the Classroom, a program run by the Constitutional Rights Foundation, which was a three time a year commitment for a one-hour class, and the Senior Center Initiative, a program by the Center for Disability and Elder Law, whereby the attorneys drafted powers of attorneys for property and health care and living wills for local low-income seniors. Both nonprofit organizations understood the West Cook model—hours and training generally take place during school hours, and the group works in pairs so that if an emergency comes up, they are covered.

Their initial trainings took place at the local library on February 25 and March 5. They were able to staff their first pro bono event in March of 2011, just two months after Donna's initial e-mail and idea. The organization now has 28 active members: one third of the group's members are solo practitioners, another one third are part-time attorneys, and the final one third are stay-at-home legal moms. Each group has a desire to do pro bono work in an efficient, closed-ended way.

> **Advice: Have a clear vision.**

The group is expanding into other areas as well. They have partnered with a local nonprofit to work on immigration cases dealing with U Visas and Violence Against Women Act applications. They are also looking at possibilities regarding tenant eviction cases with the Lawyers Committee for Better Housing and prepping victims of domestic violence for the courtroom for another nonprofit. As long as West Cook Pro Bono is able to be helpful and the project is a win-win for both organizations, they are able to make it work. If an organization wants to work with West Cook Pro Bono but won't change its training hours or allow them to work in pairs, then Donna knows that it ultimately will not work:

Know for sure what your model is, what is going to work for your participants, and what you have promised your participants. Don't feel bad about the work that needs to be done. You have to be able to say no to protect everybody.

Sheila Pont, one of the volunteers at West Cook Pro Bono Network, has been a stay-at-home legal mom of three children for fourteen years. With a joint JD/MSW from Washington University in St. Louis, Sheila began her career as an advocate for victims' families for the organization Mothers Against Drunk Driving. During her time at home, she worked on various committees and other organizations and was initially somewhat hesitant to get involved with West Cook Pro Bono. Sheila remarks,

Honestly, I didn't know if I was interested. I was very involved with other organizations. . . . I kind of felt like I was stretched pretty thin.

She sent an e-mail to Donna, and after attending the first meeting, she was hooked by the energy and enthusiasm of Donna's idea:

It had a very clear vision from the beginning. . . . Donna wanted it to be a group of people who could do nonprofit work on their own time and when they wanted to do it and that we should always be paired up . . . and the programs should always be between nine and two. She had an image of what she wanted this to look like, so it allowed us to immediately go to the next step.

Sheila has become involved as the chief organizer of the Lawyers in the Classroom project, but she has participated in other opportunities as well. She is currently working with an immigration client who is interested in pursuing a nursing degree. Sheila enjoys having a client and working through the legal issues. She describes her other experiences with West Cook Pro Bono as "incredibly positive," saying,

The work on the durable power of attorneys and the living wills was so powerful. Each interaction was only 30 to 45 minutes, but knowing that I have done that. Some of the clients were very emotional.

Being a stay-at-home mom, Sheila also enjoys the benefits of connecting with other like-minded people within her community while utilizing her legal training. She advises legal moms transitioning to stay at home: "Do everything you can to find other people to engage with on any level. . . . People who are used to being very busy, usually like being very busy." In seeking out pro bono opportunities, Sheila remarks,

> I think there are a lot of opportunities out there, but you really need to search out and find one that interests you, and you are passionate enough about, and one that fits into your schedule.

At this point, the West Cook Pro Bono Network runs on approximately $300 per year. Donna receives no payment for her organization of the group. The organization works under the auspices of the nonprofits that it serves and therefore does not need to carry malpractice insurance for its volunteers. Moreover, Donna's experience as a recruiter for the local school board has allowed her to think strategically about finding the right people who could provide low-to-no cost solutions for the group initially. For example, one of her contacts was able to design their website (http://www.westcookprobono.com/) for free. They do not have a dedicated space for the group, but Donna has considered renting a P.O. Box and plans to incorporate the group and get 501(c)(3) tax status in the next few months. The local media has also featured the network, which has helped to gain support for their programming.

Forging West Cook Pro Bono has meant so much more than helping nonprofit organizations. Local friendships have formed among the women, and it has filled a void where for many their professional life once was. Donna comments that the women are grateful for the experience:

> They are the ones who get all misty eyed when they show up with a suit on. They are so grateful to have just a couple of hours to remember that they are an independent human being who contributes to the world in a way that has nothing to do with keeping another person alive. All the things that come with being a mom are great, but it is really a tough adjustment as a professional.

On a short-term basis, Donna hopes West Cook Pro Bono becomes a group with consistent participation that is recognized for its contribution in the community. She believes it can be a catalyst for providing legal service and helping caregivers with legal degrees stay in the profession. Looking back on her interview experience after years at home with her children, Donna hopes that pro bono can provide the kind of off-ramping and on-ramping that law firms can value:

> There's not a lot geared toward keeping people in the profession. It is almost like, "Well if you want to leave, fine. And we're not going do a lot to make sure you get back in." . . . It is hard for me to believe that we as a society don't want to use that talent—people who take breaks.

For women considering a pro bono start-up, Donna first suggests finding a means to contact others in similar situations. She was able to take advantage of her local mom listserv. In her estimation, a group needs only about five people to get started. She also advises groups to start slowly and in small doses to have success initially. West Cook Pro Bono has kept up momentum by limiting meetings (only two thus far) and taking action. With one person in charge and a strong vision, Donna is able to limit competing ideas and keep her promises. She has also had a lot of support to make it work and has been able to pull in resources; from someone willing to donate time to build a website to a marketing professional who helped her choose the name. Donna comments, "I came up with this idea, but I feel very fortunate and surrounded by people who are also into finding solutions and helping." The West Cook Pro Bono Network is helping people reach professional fulfillment while contributing to the pro bono world, all because of an offhand interview question posed to Donna Peel.

THE D.C. VOLUNTEER LAWYERS PROJECT

"It has been really interesting to discover how
similar moms are everywhere."
—Jenny Brody

ACROSS THE COUNTRY IN WASHINGTON, DC, another legal mom was hitting roadblocks while trying to find a way to offer volunteer legal services. Jenny Brody graduated from Harvard Law School in 1981. After law school, she clerked for a Federal Court of Appeals judge, worked at the Department of Justice in the Civil Appellate Division, and then joined a private law firm.

In 1988, she welcomed her first child and took her first step off the traditional legal career path, negotiating a part-time arrangement, which was very unusual at the time. She had a second child in 1991 and decided to step off her career path entirely with the thought that she might return when her youngest was in kindergarten. Jenny had a third child, and fifteen years passed quickly by.

When she started to think about resurrecting her legal career, she instinctively knew that returning to traditional law firm life was not for her:

> I wanted to be a professional and use my law degree to help people, but I didn't feel like a law firm was the way I would do that. I really didn't know what to do. I was really just casting around like many people I knew in that situation. I decided to take just one pro bono case to see what I thought about it. I worked with an organization that had an office in DC. The big advantage was that they covered their volunteers with malpractice insurance.

In this initial case, Jenny represented a teenage girl who had been in the foster care system. She found the work incredibly rewarding and felt like she could make a real difference. Unfortunately, the organization under whose umbrella she worked closed its DC office. Jenny was left without malpractice insurance, but she didn't want to withdraw from representation. She made the decision to buy an individual malpractice policy, which was very expensive.

Through her passion for pro bono work, Jenny met two other attorneys in the same situation—women who had been at home for several years who were taking on pro bono cases. The genesis for the DC Volunteer Lawyers Project initially arose out of the idea that the women could get a group malpractice policy less expensively. It also helped that under DC law, inactive lawyers could represent clients in pro bono cases.

Starting in 2008, Jenny, along with Karen Barker Marcou and Marla Spindel, hosted the first organizational meeting of the DC Volunteer Lawyers Project. They advertised on local school listservs and by word of mouth, with the query, "Do you have a law degree you aren't using?" Their first meeting at Jenny's home attracted 30 lawyers. They made the decision to file for 501(c)(3) status and start an organization dedicated to supporting lawyers taking on pro bono cases primarily in areas related to family law: guardian ad litem (GAL) cases, domestic violence orders of protection, immigration, and adoption and foster parent support. Their website (http://www.dcvlp.org/index.php) describes their work:

> Founded in January of 2008, the DCVLP addresses the urgent need for more pro bono family law lawyers by tapping into an unused resource—experienced lawyers who have left full-time legal practice, many of them to raise families, and want to use their legal skills to help the community. The DCVLP assists these lawyers in reentering the legal profession by providing training programs, a professional support network, and mentorship and supervision throughout the duration of a case. The DCVLP also provides volunteers with malpractice insurance, an office for client meetings, online legal research tools and other resources they need to provide free, high-quality legal representation to indigent clients.

The greatest volume of cases for DCVLP comes from guardian ad litem and domestic violence cases. Although Jenny initially spoke with the local bar association regarding pro bono opportunities, she soon learned that obtaining cases directly from the court system was the right model for their organization. In regard to guardian ad litem cases, one of the DC Superior Court judges was very supportive in referring cases to the organization and through word of mouth, four judges on the family court have utilized DCVLP for GAL cases. As it is an area of constant need, DCVLP manages a caseload of forty to fifty open cases with ten to twenty cases on a waiting list.

In Washington, DC alone, there are more than 5,000 domestic violence protection order cases filed every year. DCVLP has filled a huge gap in advocating for victims and has been able to work directly with the court intake system to obtain clients.

In just over three years, the group has grown from three lawyers interested in reentering the profession and helping others to 540 registered volunteers. Not only does DCVLP welcome legal moms on career breaks, but it has also had great success recruiting laid-off attorneys, government attorneys, and retired lawyers. It helped their volunteer ranks that the economy turned in 2009, and job seekers were looking for ways to keep their resumes active while job searching. Being Washington, DC, the organization also had many volunteers who were not members of the DC bar association but had moved to follow a spouse's career to work in the Obama administration. DCVLP was able to petition the local court for a rule that allows non-DC lawyers to volunteer under the supervision of the organization.

Logistically, in addition to securing malpractice insurance, the organization purchased a Lexis password and set up a virtual office that gave DCVLP members an address for pleadings and access to conference rooms. The group initially had a small fundraiser to pay for malpractice insurance and the Lexis password but soon realized that for adequate growth they would need additional funding and administrative support.

> **Advice: Know when to bring on administrative support.**

They learned early that they could not expect volunteers to handle the administrative functions of the organization. In order to track caseloads and manage the volunteers, DCVLP has two full-time administrative employees and four part-time supervising attorneys. One of the supervising attorneys reviews every court document. They were able to raise enough money to hire a software professional to set up a website, database and conflict check system, which tracks all of the cases. They are also fortunate to have substantial help from interns from local colleges and universities. At this juncture, their main constraint has been raising enough funds to hire enough supervising attorneys to handle their caseloads. One of their volunteers had a business school background in addition to a law degree and was able to provide an organizational structure that has focused the founders on growing the organization and allowed the volunteers and supervising attorneys to handle individual clients. Though Jenny misses the clients, she recognizes the importance of moving the organization forward at this critical time.

The Verizon Foundation, which supports work relating to domestic violence, has awarded DCVLP grant funding. Black Entertainment Television (BET) and some private family foundations have also awarded private grants. Each year, DCVLP hosts an annual fundraiser to support the work of the organization. In March of 2010, they were awarded a Washington Area Women's Foundation Leadership Award, which came with grant funding.

The organization's initial goal was to be a group of approximately ten part-time lawyers handling twenty cases. None of the founders saw this organization growing to its current size, but they recognize that it has filled a critical need within the legal profession. Jenny comments,

> All of us who work in the organization find the work incredibly compelling and rewarding and find our clients to be rewarding to work with, so it pays back. Also there is a lot of camaraderie within our organization.

Advice: Provide opportunities to connect within the organization.

In order to promote collegiality, they schedule monthly meetings, speaker series, and active case meetings. As some of the cases can be incredibly upsetting, it is important for the lawyers to be able to connect with one another. Many of the clients are in dire circumstances, dealing with physical violence, abuse, or neglect. DCVLP gives the attorneys training to deal with the situations, but in Jenny's words, "Ultimately it is rewarding work, but it can be heartbreaking at times." She continues,

> Our volunteers ultimately feel that they are able to help these kids in a positive way, but it is also frustrating because there are not solutions to all of their problems. We can't solve the problem of poverty. So it is kind of heartrending to confront that.

Advice: Assign all cases in pairs.

In addition to their training programs in each substantive area, DCVLP took the approach of assigning all cases in pairs. In many ways, it is similar to a law firm model with a partner and associate working on a case, however for DCVLP, they have a lead counsel and shadow counsel. New volunteers are not thrown into the deep end of the pool and have the support to learn the ropes before taking a new case on their own. This model also worked for their initial group of volunteers—legal moms who had children at home whose days could be unpredictable when a child was suddenly sent home from school sick.

As they looked at other models for pro bono organizations, Jenny realized that they flipped the typical model over where agencies have staff attorneys who may not have the time to manage large groups of volunteers. DCVLP chose to focus on supporting the volunteers in order to reach a critical mass of clients who desperately need services. At times they have had too many volunteers in need of training and have found creative solutions, such as putting their training programs online courtesy of a local film school. Attorney volunteers are also able to access a password-protected pleadings database to assist in drafting court documents. Jenny comments, "It turns out you can run a big legal operation now without a real bricks and mortar office."

Advice: Getting back into the profession may require confidence building.

At this point, Jenny estimates that one third of the volunteers are stay-at-home legal moms on career break. With so many volunteers who have been out of law practice, they initially found the group needed to build confidence. Some of their early meetings started with the introduction, "Hi, my name is _____, and I have been out of law practice for 10 years." Jenny notes,

> The biggest challenge we faced initially when it was an organization just of moms on career break was the problem of confidence. Because we found that all of us, including those of us who founded the organization, after staying home and being out of legal practice for a long time really had trepidation about rejoining the professional world or functioning as lawyers and professionals again. . . . Initially, we really functioned as a support group in the sense of realizing that we can still be lawyers. We can regain skills. We can learn new skills. We can learn new substantive areas of law. . . . We can be effective advocates for our clients and get good results in court. We had to convince ourselves of that.

Despite this challenge, at least two thirds of the volunteers return to take on new cases. The organization provides skills and resume building for attorneys trying to reenter the workforce. It also can serve as a reference. Some of the volunteers have enjoyed the work so immensely they have started their own solo family law practices. For those who aren't looking to reenter the legal profession in a paid capacity, it has given them a bridge to the professional world. Jenny comments, "It is really important to them to keep their professional skills intact and just be able to use their law degree in a constructive way." She can certainly relate. Having been home with her own children for fifteen years, she missed having a professional identity.

Jenny advises other women interested in the model provided by the DCVLP to go for it! She would love to act as a resource for other women interested in starting similar programs. She remarks, "We think our model could be replicated in other cities."

Jenny envisions securing additional funding so that the organization can hire more supervising attorneys and take on more cases, but currently with the tremendous growth that they have had, sometimes they are just trying to get through each week. She is encouraged by the volunteers who have gotten so much out of the experience:

> Great volunteers can be any age, any stage of life, any gender. The lawyers that volunteer with us find it extremely rewarding. In addition, because they have the resources they need, they feel confident that they can handle the case.

Chapter Twenty-One

THE WORK-FROM-HOME LEGAL MOM

"Listen to your heart. I don't feel like I am ever going to look back and regret being with my kids."
—Gwen Norgle-Reedy

GWEN NORGLE-REEDY GREW UP as the youngest of nine children in a family where law was in their blood. In her words, "I come from a very legal family. It was kind of like our family business." She saw her father run successful campaigns for the judiciary as a child and eventually be appointed as a federal judge when she was ten years old. It is no surprise that of the nine children, five have gone on to careers as lawyers.

Knowing that law was her likely career path, as an undergraduate Gwen attended the University of Notre Dame and subsequently enrolled in IIT Chicago-Kent College of Law. During law school, she clerked for a sole practitioner who primarily focused in litigation. After graduation, Gwen joined as an associate. The firm had grown, and the attorney had also taken on two partners. Gwen worked in litigation doing trial work and arbitration. She comments,

> I had a lot of front line experience where I was given a lot of responsibility and learned how to fend for myself in a lot of ways. . . . I was

doing everything from creating invoices to cross examining witnesses at trial. I learned a lot about how to run a small business and also how to co-chair a trial.

After three years at the firm, Gwen knew she was ready for a change. She took contract jobs with larger firms for about a year while she tried to find her way into a position with the government. Initially, she took a pro bono position with the government in the hopes that a full-time job would become available. Eventually, she was taken on as a contract employee, working for the agency as her contract was continually renewed. She enjoyed the work and saw her future there.

After two years, she was offered her dream job—a full-time position with benefits doing work that she wanted to do. Unfortunately, the job was out of state and would require her and her husband to move, or for her to commute on weekends back to their home in Chicago. Because her husband was a third-generation realtor in a family business, moving was not conducive to his career. Gwen made the difficult decision to turn down the offer.

Around the same time, Gwen and her husband decided that they wanted to start a family. With five years of law practice behind her, she was struggling with where her career was versus where she thought it might be:

> I realized that I might not be hitting the marks in my career where I wanted to be when I had kids. . . . I wasn't feeling the desire to have my kids at the same time as my career track was going. When I got to the point when I kind of thought biologically I should start having kids, I was at a point in my career when I was very, very close to hitting my dream job. I think that was frustrating for me because I knew that I had to make a choice between climbing this mountain of my dream job or starting to settle in and sacrificing some of my career goals.

After learning she was pregnant, Gwen was offered another job with the government through a referral. She started the position while pregnant. Though she enjoyed the work, after having her daughter she realized that her heart was at home. Using her time off and remote work arrangements, Gwen was able to be at home two days of the week and in the office three days. She hoped to make a part-time arrangement more formal.

She spoke very candidly with her boss and requested a part-time schedule. Her request was rejected, which she understood, being a relatively new hire for the agency. She made the decision to leave the job but said that she would stay until they found a replacement. While in the process of leaving the job, beginning to decrease her caseload and gradually moving out of her office, she received word of an opportunity to work from home. After receiving a job offer, she gave her two-week's notice with the government. Ironically, at that point, the government offered her a part-time position, but she couldn't turn down the work-from-home opportunity.

With her six-month-old daughter at home, Gwen began her work-from-home legal career for a transportation services company. The general counsel started the remote work program approximately ten years earlier with the idea that the work would be contracted from the in-house headquarters. With seven attorneys on staff working remotely, many of them are moms who left conventional law firms and corporations.

Gwen had to undergo training for the job, for which she essentially performs contract review assignments. She has a high level of responsibility:

> There is an understanding that this is a professional relationship. There has to be trust that the work will get done when it is due to be completed.

Generally, she is given a five-day turnaround for most assignments. She can also take rush assignments when her schedule allows. In her interview, a supervisor did ask whether she had childcare in the event she was crunched on an assignment. In Gwen's opinion, it was a valid question considering the circumstances of the work situation.

Advice: Be extremely diligent about tracking your work time.

Typically, Gwen works the night shift. After bedtime, she starts working by 8:00 or 9:00. She might also have a few minutes during the day if the kids are napping. Sometimes she works outside of gymnastics class with a contract, a highlighter, and a pen. Gwen actually uses a stopwatch while she is working to track her time. This allows her to compartmentalize and give the company the full value of her time. Because she invoices the company every two weeks, she needs to keep very detailed track of her time on a daily basis.

Gwen is also careful not to convey any home-related issues to the client, generally the business development department of the company. There is an understanding that she is a professional. She schedules conference calls far enough in advance so that she can get a babysitter if necessary. It helps that her husband has an alternative work schedule and a day off in the middle of the week. She remarks, "I don't ever really advertise that I am a stay-at-home mom."

With her children aged 3 1/2 and 18 months, Gwen can reflect on her experience working from home for the last three years. She has been able to be present for her children's developmental moments: first steps, first solid food, and so forth. If one of the kids has a rough night, Gwen doesn't have the pressure to put on a suit and get out to the office. She hasn't had to pump milk extensively, and she can role with the demands of the day. Essentially, Gwen is able to be there for her children's immediate needs.

Gwen also credits working from home with allowing her to be efficient, both at work and in her family life. Without a two-hour commute, childcare issues, or worrying about office facetime, Gwen can devote herself completely to the work at hand:

> My work is better because I don't have to get on a train or sit in a car and get to an office. I can be more focused because I am switching gears quickly. There is no wasted time. I don't have to put makeup on and make sure I have a clean shirt.

Gwen considers support from her husband as critical in helping her make it all work. Because he doesn't have a traditional 9:00 to 5:00 job, he is able to take the morning shift with the kids. This allows her to sleep a little later when she has been up late working. He can also come home from the office when she needs to make an important phone call. Gwen is also fortunate to have family nearby to help when she needs an occasional babysitter. She uses other strategies, like online grocery shopping, to streamline the tasks that need to get done:

> For me the work doesn't suffer. It's the house. Maybe there's a little more pizza than homemade food, but they do eat healthy. The work never suffers, but I am in my pajamas instead of a suit.

Working the day shift at home and the night shift in her home office can pose some challenges. Specifically to Gwen, compartmentalizing can be an issue. There were times when the kids were painting or when she was nursing and her mind would wander to the thought that if she couldn't get any work done during the day, she would need to pull an all-nighter. She needs to keep pace with her work and the deadlines weigh on her. In her words, "There are so many hours of the day, and some of those hours are going to have to go into the wee hours of the night." Lack of sleep is just a part of life.

Gwen can remember particularly challenging times during her busy season at work when both children were sick. Trying to keep it together at home while making sure she was getting her work done made for sleepless nights and extra coffee. She got through it by knowing that everything comes in phases:

> I know this is only temporary. I think that is what keeps me sane. These are special times with them being little and being here for all their developmental moments. I know this is only temporary. I see other women who have come out of this phase.

Gwen actually sees many moms in her neighborhood in similar situations, working part-time schedules as insurance agents, real estate agents, or nurses. From Gwen's perspective, she doesn't really miss going out into the work world at this point: "I feel like I get that sense of being out in the world when I open up my computer at night and use my brain and review legal issues and articulate in a memo suggested modifications to a contract."

In her current position, Gwen is able to bring home a paycheck and stay in the game. Her resume has been active, and she has had precious time with her children. In looking back on her career before children, she thinks she should have made the switch to the government sooner so she might have built up her desired career for a longer amount of time:

> I was peaking in my career at the same time as I was starting to long for children. I wish I would have peaked in my career a little sooner before I left. I feel like I am in a niche with my resume and my career that will allow me to get back into the game when the time is right for my family.

Advice: Let others know you are looking for work-from-home opportunities.

In Gwen's opinion, working from home within the law is a good option for women who want to spend time at home while their children are young. She notes, "I think my situation is unique, but I know that there are opportunities out there." For women who would like to follow a similar path, Gwen suggests networking with others to find out about their experiences, including those in local bar associations. She also recommends speaking with women in other professions who have found a work-at-home niche that might be applicable to the legal profession. She advises getting the word out about trying to find a work-from-home opportunity. She was able to find her current job through a referral from a friend who was in the same situation. There may also be opportunities to piece together contract legal work from multiple sources.

Of her legal mom peers in the profession, Gwen has seen all sides of work-life balance; female partners with three children, corporate attorneys with children, and women working part time. Of the legal moms with whom she primarily associates, most of them are part time or working remotely—further evidence that there are such options within the law, despite those in the profession who say it can't be done. To such naysayers, Gwen recalls forming her own opinion on the subject:

> To me, when I was pregnant with my first daughter and I was working and people were telling me, "No, you can't do this job from home or with an alternative work schedule." I respectfully disagreed. I never really fought back too much, but in my head, I said, "Well, if this is not the right thing for this position for what they think they want, then I am going to find it somewhere else."

Gwen would advise women considering a career in the law to look at all possibilities within the profession, keeping in mind that a family-friendly environment is important. From her perspective, there are numerous ways to find a fulfilling career in the law:

> Explore all the opportunities that the law has to offer. Do not get pigeonholed into what you think a lawyer is. I thought a lawyer was somebody who was in the courtroom. . . . That was fulfilling for me and I am glad that have that experience, but there are many different types of lawyers out there who do wonderful things.

She also recommends that each woman finds what her passion is and tries to connect it to a career path, particularly before going too far down a professional road toward something less optimal. It may help to find mentors or women in the profession to emulate. Gwen notes, "Find people who are happy with their careers. Find role models." She also cautions women not to let someone tell you what is not possible. In her situation, working from home has been entirely possible. With advances in technology, there are more ways to do legal work from home. This may cut down on water cooler conversations, but on the other hand, it can also create efficiency.

Looking at her own legal family, Gwen can say that her siblings working in the law are where they want to be. Her sisters who are legal moms have also been able to carve out part-time or work-from-home options. One of her brothers has also worked out an alternative work schedule related to parenting responsibilities.

Perhaps when her children are in school, Gwen will go back to work outside her home, maybe even back to the government. Of one thing she is certain: "I want to be behind a cause and a mission. I don't think I just want to be billing time or in litigation." As any mom knows, legal or not, time is precious, spent at work or at home. Gwen has been able to find the right balance for her and her young family while working in the law.

Chapter Twenty-Two

A MOM'S VIEW
FROM THE BENCH

"I have the perfect job."

—*The Honorable Patricia A. Gaughan, U.S. District Court for the*
Northern District of Ohio, Eastern Division

ARGUABLY, BEING A FEDERAL JUDGE might be the optimal job for a legal
working mom. Good salary? Check. Good benefits? Check. Interesting
work? Check. Reasonable hours? Check. Job Security? Well, it is a lifetime appointment, so that simply goes without saying.

The more difficult problem for a legal mom who wants this job is
how to actually be appointed as a Federal Judge by the President of the
United States. . . . Details, details . . .

Judge Patricia Gaughan of the U.S. District Court for the Northern
District of Ohio did not originally have her sights set on being a judge
nor was she certain she even wanted to be an attorney. At St. Mary's
College of Notre Dame, Judge Gaughan majored in Business and Political Science. She ultimately wanted a career in the business world. She
was accepted to the Northwestern School of Management and to Notre
Dame Law School. She comments on her plans at the time:

I had applied to law school because I was told that a law degree would
get me just as far, if not further, in business than a business degree. I
really intended to use my law degree for business.

Ultimately, Judge Gaughan chose to pursue law school, in great
measure because she didn't want to leave Notre Dame. Entering law
school, she definitely intended to go into business as a career. Two
courses, Evidence and Criminal Law, changed her mind. She also credits her moot court trial division team as a major influence in guiding her
decision. She remarks, "I absolutely fell in love with trial work and the
criminal side of law." Based on these experiences, she knew she had to
be a trial lawyer.

Upon law school graduation, Judge Gaughan received a job offer to
be an Assistant U.S. Attorney in Hammond, Indiana, but unfortunately
the funding for the position had not come through, so she returned to
her hometown of Cleveland, Ohio to wait for word. Wisely, she had
taken both the Indiana Bar Exam and the Ohio Bar Exam with the
thought that she might return to Ohio in the future.

As she grew weary of waiting to hear from Hammond, she decided
to send some resumes out in Cleveland. Within a short time, she
received offers from both the Cuyahoga County Prosecutor's Office
and the Cuyahoga County Public Defender's Office. As the funding
from the federal government for the position in Hammond had still not
come through, she made the decision to take a job with the Criminal
Division of the Cuyahoga County Prosecutor's Office. Ironically, the
funding for the federal position came through 30 days later, but Judge
Gaughan didn't feel right leaving the job and came to love working in
the Prosecutor's office.

She loved the position and worked her way up to become the first
woman assigned to the Major Trial Division where she worked on rape,
murder, and political corruption cases. After nearly 5 years, she left to
join the United States Attorney's Office. Though she valued the experience, after a year she decided to pursue an opportunity to do civil work,
becoming affiliated with a firm. During that time, she was able to continue her work with the Cuyahoga County Prosecutor's Office—giving
her a foot in each door, both civil and criminal work.

Judge Gaughan's range of experience would suggest that she was
headed for the judiciary, but it was not even in the back of her mind,

and in her words, "Nobody believes it." She had no plans to pursue the judiciary as she was happy with her work. She explains what changed her mind:

> I appeared in front of a couple of judges that made me say to myself, that is not how I would have handled it had I been a judge, and I think I could maybe do a better job. That is what put the spark in me.

In 1986, she ran for the Cuyahoga County Court of Common Pleas. She won the Democratic Primary against two male opponents and then faced a Republican woman in the General Election. She won the race and took office January 7, 1987. In 1992, she ran for election again, and was ultimately unopposed.

In 1995, Senator John Glenn of Ohio put together a commission to interview applicants for a federal judgeship, which was opening when Judge Ann Aldrich decided to take senior status. Judge Aldrich had been the first female judge in the Federal District Court for the Northern District of Ohio. Judge Gaughan applied and was chosen for an interview. The commission submitted three names to Senator Glenn. Judge Gaughan was ranked first among the candidates. Senator Glenn called her to tell her the happy news and submitted her name to President Clinton. On December 22, 1995, the United States Senate confirmed her, and she received her commission on December 26, 1995. Reflecting on her appointment, she comments, "I was so nervous that I don't think I appreciated it all at the time."

Judge Gaughan's career is certainly impressive, but the fact that she was able to juggle two children as she ascended within the judiciary is remarkable. She was engaged in 1986 when she first ran for Common Pleas judge. They were married in 1987, and Judge Gaughan relates, "We struggled to get pregnant." In a twist of fate, someone approached her husband to act as the attorney to find adoptive parents for a young woman who was planning to put her child up for adoption. He responded that rather than taking on her case, he and his wife would be interested in being considered. In another twist of fate, after the agreement of adoption, but before they physically had their son, Judge Gaughan learned she was pregnant. In 1989, they adopted their son, and 8 months later in 1990, they welcomed their daughter. Judge Gaughan relates her feelings at the time:

It was the absolute happiest time of my life. You know how they talk about postpartum depression, I had the opposite problem. I was higher than a kite. I was just euphoric because I had these two fabulous babies, a boy and a girl, eight and a half months apart. I look at them as my miracles.

> **Advice: Make lifestyle choices that will support your roles.**

Judge Gaughan became a mother 2 years and a few months after taking the bench. She was determined to make it all work. They chose a house as close to downtown Cleveland as possible so that she was within a 15-minute drive if she needed to get home for the kids. She also made the decision to hire someone to come into her home to care for the children. In her words, her babysitter was the "warmest, most wonderful person." She further relates,

> I was determined that I wanted somebody to come into my house. I didn't want to have to wake them up in the morning. I didn't want to have to take them out. . . . It gave me an incredible sense of peace that they were in such wonderful hands. So that made the adjustment easy. I did find that I would go home and spend every minute with them until they fell asleep, and then I pulled my briefcase out. It was a lot of work, but I was so euphoric that it didn't feel like work.

Her workday started at 8:00 a.m. and was all about docket control. She was very organized with her schedule in order to manage the workload. Despite the demands on her time, she tried to be home no later than 5:30; however, like many legal working moms, she comments, "I always pulled out my briefcase after the kids went to bed." Judge Gaughan particularly relates how important her own personal work ethic was to her own peace of mind:

> I was a very hard worker, and I was very conscious of my docket and always staying on top of it. I was also conscious of never letting a law clerk, for example, do a settlement conference or a status conference. I always did that myself because I believe very strongly lawyers deserve to see the judge and not a law clerk, with no disrespect to a law clerk.

Judge Gaughan also held the attitude that the courtroom was the forum for the litigants, taking her responsibility to the people whom she served very seriously:

> Some judges have the attitude, "It is my courtroom. It is my time. We start when I get there, not when I scheduled it." I don't take that attitude and I don't think that is fair to attorneys. . . . That's an important point for me. I never wanted my children to suffer because of my job, but on the other hand, I couldn't live with myself if I ever felt I was less of a judge because I was giving too much on the other side.

Because she did work so hard on the job, she was comfortable carving out time in her schedule when she needed to do so for playground duty, field trips, or doctor's appointments. In her position of authority, she had more control over her schedule than a typical practicing attorney. She notes, "I was just so fortunate that I had the type of job that I could take off a couple of hours." Having a balanced home life and work life ultimately made her a happier person all around:

> I was a happier judge and a happier mom because I was able to do both, so I just didn't feel guilty. . . . I felt that I was able to do both and have a good conscience about the manner in which I did both. It was very important to me that I felt that way.

Advice: Know what works for you.

Judge Gaughan particularly did not have the feelings of guilt that many working mothers describe. She was well established in her career, enjoyed her work, and loved being a mother. She also knew what worked for her:

> The reason I didn't [feel guilty] is because I know myself. I know I was a better mother because when I went home, I wanted to be there. I wanted to spend every minute with them. I can say, not boasting, but as a matter of fact, that my children know that they are more important to me than life itself. They never felt a moment of not being loved. I never felt that I was taking anything away from them. . . . Having my job and then just devoting all my free time to the kids while they were awake made me so happy that I never felt dissatisfied.

I never felt like maybe there is something else that I am missing out on. I was just so happy, and I know my happiness reflected on to them. I really believe that.

Her greatest challenge in balancing work and family came when she campaigned for reelection in 1992. Her children were still toddlers and all of her work related to the election had to take place in the evenings and weekends. It required her to be out and about, but she also had to focus on campaign literature, fundraising, and getting mailings out. Fortunately, once the filing deadline passed, she learned that she was running unopposed, and she could ease up on some of her appearances:

Campaigning is just rough. If you do it the right way, you are out every night. That is why I was just so blessed when I didn't have opposition.

Despite the demands of the campaign, Judge Gaughan still strived to be with her children as much as possible. She describes the scene of the campaign:

I allowed them to be around while we were doing it. I didn't just lock myself in a room and not let them see me because I thought that was important. . . . We would be there working while they were playing. So at least my physical presence was there.

In addition to having a trusted caregiver for her children during the day, Judge Gaughan also credits the support of her parents, sisters, and especially her husband, who also acted as her campaign manager. She notes, "Without the partnership I had with my husband, I don't know if I could have done it." She describes him as a modern father, willing to take on responsibilities at home as well. His support was a key to her success:

We really are partners. You hear of some men that couldn't handle a spouse making more money. My husband couldn't care less. . . . He is just an incredibly secure, confident man who views our marriage as a partnership.

Judge Gaughan was also faced with additional challenges that are not typical to most legal moms. Both as a Common Pleas and Federal judge, she received death threats. When she was at the hospital delivering her daughter, she had to be put in a private room with a security guard because of a recent death threat. In addition, she keeps a picture of a man on her desk who tried to hire someone to kill her from prison. On another occasion, she was outside her home with the children when a car drove by very slowly, taking pictures with a long-range lens. She ran after the car to get the license number. All of the incidents were dealt with by the police and United States Marshall Service and never amounted to anything. However, it affected her sisters and certainly made her more protective of her children. She comments on the incidents, "I didn't care about myself. It was my children."

Despite the rigors of campaigning and the death threats, Judge Gaughan has loved her work in the judiciary and considers herself very fortunate to be part of the federal system. Her children were 6 and 7 when she was appointed to the federal bench. She acknowledges the security that comes with having a lifetime appointment, which does not require her to continually campaign. In her words, "This is a lifetime job. Yes, I can make my own hours. There just isn't the spotlight on our individual dockets because we don't run."

Her position has given her the balanced work and family life that she so wanted. As an employer, she is keenly aware of the demands placed on working parents. Although she has always worked full time, she has never taken for granted that if her child had to go the doctor, she could take off an hour and not have to answer to anyone.

> I am very, very conscious of people who aren't as fortunate as I am, and I feel like I have to help them out because I have had such an incredibly wonderful career where all the stars properly aligned for me to get this position, that this is my way of giving back and saying okay, I know you weren't as lucky as I am to get this job, but I am going to make it as family friendly as possible.

To this effect, in 1988 she made a significant contribution to the lives of working parents in the Common Pleas Court by championing job sharing. Her trusted bailiff came to her and related that though she loved the job, she needed to spend more time at home with her family. Judge Gaughan empathized with her situation and did not want to lose her as a key staff person. She asked her if she might be interested in doing the job on a part-time basis if she could figure out a job-sharing situation. Judge Gaughan consulted the administrative judge for the court, who was reticent, but ultimately left the decision up to her. As the first judge to support job sharing, women from the probation department and court reporters soon approached her, asking her to back their request for job sharing. She wrote a proposed policy and presented it to the personnel committee. It was very controversial at the time, but the measure was put through allowing job sharing with some restrictions.

> I have felt very fortunate that being a judge, I have at least made a contribution to effecting change in the court systems. . . . Women were craving some alternatives. They needed someone to say, "Come on, it's time."

When she moved to the federal court, Judge Gaughan was able to bring over the job-sharing situation with her. She also allows her law clerks to job share. The federal court has been much more progressive, allowing some employees to work from home in a limited teleworking arrangement. Those who have taken advantage of the flexible workplace policies over the years have been incredibly grateful to Judge Gaughan for her support.

> I am so fortunate that I am able as an employer to be very conscious of the needs, not only of women, but of men too. . . . I am so grateful that I have been in the position to champion that.

In her opinion, the legal profession generally is not as reasonable in its demands of working parents. Generally, law firms are concerned about the bottom line and don't necessarily respect people wanting a good balance.

> I don't think our profession is particularly kind to men and women who want to have a good balance between work and family. I wish our profession would take a serious look at it, but I am just not optimistic because it goes back to profit and billable hours.

On one occasion, Judge Gaughan called an older male partner at a law firm as a reference for a potential law clerk. He indicated that the woman would be wonderful for the job, not only because she was very bright but also because she would never be on partnership track because she wanted to have kids. It bothered Judge Gaughan, and she remembers hoping that her own generation and those after would have a different attitude. Had the tables been turned and it was a male attorney who wanted to be her law clerk, it is unlikely that the partnership prospects for that male attorney would have been dashed if he decided he wanted to have children. Judge Gaughan further notes,

> I have a stack of resumes from women in the bigger firms wanting to be a law clerk and take a significant cut in pay, and I believe it is in great measure because of the hours that are required of them. I think they have a hard time juggling motherhood with the profession when they are required to put in so many billable hours. They are required to be there on weekends. Women get to the point where they say that the quality of life is just not there. I have seen women leave the profession if they can't find something.

Judge Gaughan has also tried to be accommodating to the work-life balance concerns of attorneys who have appeared in her courtroom. Recently, when scheduling trial starts in the morning, it came to her attention that one of the male attorneys had to take his children to school on his way into downtown. Rather than push the early start time, it was no problem to get started at 9:00. She has accommodated other requests as well, be they medical or family issues. She simply understands that the law can be a more reasonable place to work:

> It saddens me that people in this profession, be it attorneys, partners, or judges, who are in a position to help be more family friendly [aren't]—it is very depressing and discouraging to me that we aren't and we should be.

In her opinion, Judge Gaughan does not see this issue as exclusive to women. She remarks, "We have got to start helping both men and women juggle." As human beings, we have to be aware of the importance of work-life balance. Unfortunately, Judge Gaughan is not optimistic about the state of legal profession in this regard:

> I think women have to make a concerted effort to change the mind-set of men. Women have to get into the big law firms, get into the position of authority, and change the culture. But I am so pessimistic about what I see, in good conscience I don't know if I could say to my daughter or my good friend's daughter, "Go the big law firm route and get to be a partner and you change things."

Judge Gaughan has found her place within the legal profession and has changed the working culture along the way. She acknowledges that being in a position of authority has made it easier for her to balance, but cautions those who set out to be a judge that it is a hard road:

> It is very difficult to set out to be a judge. So many factors have to come into play. Everything has to fit very neatly. You have to do a lot of groundwork once you make the decision—a lot of groundwork. You have to get in the right race, because it is still a name game.

Advice: Being a judge is a job, not simply a title.

As a judge, she is constantly faced with difficult, life-changing issues for the litigants in her courtroom. She has to sentence people to prison and face the victims who are crying before her. She does not take these responsibilities lightly and advises anyone who aspires to the judiciary to think long and hard about it:

> If you want the title, you are not going to be a good judge. . . . This is a job and you should want the job and everything that comes with the job. Forget about the title. You are no better than anyone else, you just have a different job.

There were days when she had to make a conscious effort on her drive home to think through the stresses and issues of her day and get through them so that she could be 100% for her children when she arrived at home:

> We are human beings. Some decisions are just tough. . . . I would always say, "Look, you worked through it. It wasn't a knee-jerk decision. You just have got to let this go." I would talk myself through it on the drive home.

With 8 years on the Common Pleas bench and 17 years on the federal bench, Judge Gaughan maintains that she has the "perfect job." It may allow a degree of reasonableness in work-life balance not always found within the law, but it also comes with the challenges of campaigning, the possibility of death threats, and the certainty of having to make difficult decisions—all important concerns to be weighed by any legal mom considering a road to the judiciary.